Chrysanthemums

Chrysanthemums
AND OTHER STORIES

FENG JICAI

*Translated from the Chinese and
with an Introduction by
Susan Wilf Chen*

Harcourt Brace Jovanovich, Publishers
San Diego   New York   London

The stories in this volume first appeared between 1979 and 1983 in various Chinese literary magazines as follows: "The Mao Button": "Xiangzhang," *Wenyi zhoukan* (Tianjin: Tianjin ribaoshe) 1980, no. 4: 4–8; "Chrysanthemums": "Diaohua yandou," *Dangdai* (Beijing: Renmin wenxue chubanshe), 1979, no. 2: 76–85; "Numbskull": "Wo zheige bendan!" *Changcheng* (Shijiazhuang: Changcheng zazhi she), 1980, no. 5 (this edition inaccessible for page reference); "The Hornets' Nest": "Tong mafengwo," *Shouhuo* (Shanghai: Shanghai wenyi chubanshe), 1983, no. 2: 129–30; "A letter": "Ah!" *Shouhuo* (Shanghai: Shanghai wenyi chubanshe), 1979, no. 6: 4–38; "Plum Blossoms in the Snow": "Dou han tu," *Xingang* (Tianjin: Xingang wenyi yuekan she), 1980, no. 4: 4–25; "Winding Brook Way": "Hewan meile," *Beijing wenxue* (Beijing: Beijing wenxue yuekan she), 1981, no. 8: 29–31; "Nectar": "Jiu de moli," *Xiaoshuo jie* (Shanghai: Shanghai wenyi chubanshe), 1981, no. 1: 123–129; "The Street-Sweeping Show": "Biaoyan saodi," *Yuhua* (Nanjing: Jiangsu renmin chubanshe), 1982, no. 8: 34–36.

All but three of the stories in this volume have been reprinted in Feng's four story collections: *Feng Jicai zhong duanpian xiaoshuo ji* (The collected stories of Feng Jicai) (Beijing: Zhongguo qingnian chubanshe, 1981); *Diaohua yandou* (The carved pipe) (Guangzhou: Guangdong renmin chubanshe, 1981); *Yidali xiaotiqin* (The Italian violin) (Tianjin: Baihua wenyi chubanshe, 1982); and *Gao nüren he tade ai zhangfu* (The tall woman and her short husband) (Shanghai: Shanghai wenyi chubanshe, 1984).

Three of the translations in this volume were originally published in slightly different form as follows: "Chrysanthemums": "The Carved Pipe," *Chinese Literature* (Beijing), 1983, no. 9: 27–48; "Winding Brook Way": "Just a Spot Somewhere . . ." *The Christian Science Monitor*, 18 May 1983: 21; "The Street-Sweeping Show": *Stone Lion Review* 11 (1983): 85–89.

LIBRARY OF CONGRESS CATALOGING IN PUBLICATION DATA

Feng, Chi-ts'ai.
  Chrysanthemums and other stories.
  Contents: Chrysanthemums—Numbskull—The hornets'
nest—The Mao button—[etc.]
  1. Feng, Chi-ts'ai—Translations, English. I. Title.
PL2857.E516A23 1985   895.1'35   85-925
ISBN 0-15-117878-X

Designed by Michael Farmer

Printed in the United States of America

First edition

A B C D E

For Daying

CONTENTS

ACKNOWLEDGMENTS

I am deeply grateful to all those who helped me complete this book. Professor Patrick Hanan encouraged me to undertake the project and provided inspiration and guidance at every stage of writing. My parents, Ruth and Herbert Wilf; my grandparents, Bernice and Henry Tumen; my aunt, Ruth Potsdamer; and my brothers, David and Peter Wilf, read the manuscript critically and offered encouragement and many valuable suggestions.

Sarah Queen provided me with the photo of Feng Jicai on the jacket, which was taken by the Tianjin photographer Wu Jinghua. My parents-in-law, Chen Sibo and He Qianying, helped me get in touch with Feng. Margaret Decker interviewed Feng for me in Tianjin in the summer of 1982 and gave me the Chinese text of her interview.

For reading and commenting on the translations, obtaining rare materials, explaining difficult passages, or offering expert advice, I would like to thank Professors

Cyril Birch, Howard Hibbett, James R. Hightower, Leo Ou-fan Lee, Perry Link, Margaret Sung, Tang Yijie, Wei-ming Tu, and Yue Daiyun; and Inger McCabe Elliott, James Feinerman, Carma Hinton, Shou-ying L. Lin, Peter Michelson, Julia Murray, Wang Yihua, and Zhu Zhai. My thanks also go to John E. Woods for his perceptive editing of the manuscript.

Special thanks are due to Feng Jicai for his enthusiastic assistance. He has corresponded with me regularly and sent me his stories and photographs of his paintings. He has also made minor revisions—mostly deletions—in some of his stories to enhance their appeal for Western readers. In one case the revision was substantial: the deletion of a long flashback at the beginning of "A Letter" so that the English translation would open with the main action of the story.

I remain solely responsible for the selection of the stories and the contents of the introduction.

Susan Wilf Chen

Chrysanthemums

INTRODUCTION

Feng Jicai is one of the outstanding writers of short fiction in China today. Like the best of his contemporaries, he presents an unvarnished, often stark picture of Chinese life. But Feng does more than expose Chinese political and social ills. With rare artistry and insight into human nature, he depicts the Chinese experience in universal human terms.

Feng was born in 1942 in Tianjin, where he lives now with his wife and son.[1] He was one of six children in a wealthy family; his father owned a bank, a mine, and a wheat mill, and his mother was an artistically inclined woman from a family of highly placed civil servants.

1. In addition to the sources cited below, my account of Feng's life is based on Xie Daguang, "Gelouli de zuojia" (Writer in a garret), *Wenhui yuekan*, 1983, no. 7: 30–35; and Feng Jicai, "Tantan wode 'sanjitiao'" (My "three leaps"), *Guangzhou wenyi*, 1980, no. 10: 67–69.

The sheltered circumstances of Feng's youth freed him for intellectual pursuits. According to one of his friends, he was a naive, sentimental dreamer who lived in a fantasy world of poetry, painting, and music. As Feng himself has put it, "My world before the tumult of 1966 was like the calm before the storm: there was no sign of what the future held. . . ."[2]

He was a creative, talented, and mischievous child, an undistinguished student, but a passionate poet and artist. While still in high school he made a traditional Chinese painting that won a prize in a citywide competition. Upon graduation from high school he decided on a career as a painter and applied to the Central Academy of Fine Arts:

Dedicated to the pursuit of beauty, I made up my mind to devote my life to the palette. Boats in the rain, birds on branches, little flowers and plants in the earth . . . bound me to my easel, and I never dreamed of leaving it again.[3]

Feng, who is over six feet tall, has always been an excellent basketball player. Just as he was about to go to Beijing to take the second round of entrance exams for the Central Academy of Fine Arts, he happened to be spotted by the coach of the Tianjin Men's Basketball

2. Feng Jicai, "Mingyun de qushi" (The call of fate), *Wenyi bao*, 1981, no. 6: 38.
3. Ibid.

Team, who urged him to abandon his career plans in art and join the team. Feng felt obliged to accept the offer, largely because his mother was afraid that if he went to art school he would be sent away to teach after graduation, whereas playing basketball would enable him to stay in Tianjin.

Although Feng enjoyed playing professional basketball, he missed literature and art intensely. On his days off he hurried home to paint, and at night in the team dormitory, while his teammates slept, he forced himself to stay awake and read. He finally resigned from the team because of numerous injuries and returned gladly to painting, his chosen vocation.

He got a job in the Tianjin Calligraphy and Painting Society making copies, for export, of ancient paintings, but found the work stifling. As an outlet for his intellectual energy he studied local history and folk art, and often rode his bicycle around Tianjin collecting samples of local art.

Had it not been for the Cultural Revolution, Feng would probably have continued this life of placid artistic pursuits and intellectual browsing. As he has put it, "Like a bolt from the blue, the sudden chaos of 1966 brought my world crashing down around my ears."[4] One summer day in that year he was accosted in the street by Red Guards, who chopped his hair off; he hurried home only to find more Red Guards ransacking his father's house. Feng's treasured collection of books and art was de-

4. Ibid.

stroyed. His father's house was confiscated, and Feng was compelled to marry his fiancée hastily just so that they would be allotted a place to live. After the marriage, however, the couple was shunted from one cramped apartment to another.

He began to experience financial hardship for the first time. The source of his father's income was cut off, and Feng and his colleagues were unable to continue to earn a living by copying traditional paintings, which were now deemed counterrevolutionary. Eventually they turned to making silkscreened armbands and Chairman Mao portraits, and printing labels on plastic bags of candy and machine parts. One of Feng's jobs was to ride his bicycle from factory to factory to sell the bags. He also worked in a handicrafts factory and taught art at an elementary school.

Feng began secretly to write fiction during the Cultural Revolution. He has recently explained that painting —which in Chinese aesthetics is concerned exclusively with beautiful or restful subject matter (Feng refers to this fact in "Winding Brook Way")—seemed an inadequate means of expression during those troubled times. Only words, he felt, could accommodate the range of feelings and ideas he wanted to express.

Feng recalls that it was the "intensity of the horror" of the Cultural Revolution that moved him to begin to write.[5] He made a conscious decision to try to re-create

5. Peter Michelson, "Cultural Scars: Feng Jicai Interview," *Rolling Stock* 3 (Summer 1982): 14.

the experience in fiction for his descendants. He believes that "in a sense catastrophe is fortunate for a writer of fiction,"[6] because it provides inspiration and reveals the inner thoughts of all kinds of people who would normally remain a mystery. Here is his description of the kind of experience that inspired him to write his first stories:

> There's a place by the Hai River in Tianjin called Guajiasi, where a few swimmers drown every summer; their bodies are fished out and laid on the banks until their relatives come to claim them. But during the Cultural Revolution people committed suicide there practically every day; they were dragged out of the river with grappling hooks and laid out in rows on the banks. The couple of mats they had there were not enough, and some of the ghastly faces were left exposed. There were young ones, old ones, and women who had drowned themselves with their babies strapped to their waists. As I stared in shock at these people who had resolved to take their own lives, I imagined what they had been through. Once I noticed scuff marks of indecision on the chair that someone had used to hang himself. The sight filled me with fear and trembling. Whenever I saw something like this I would unconsciously try to fabricate the story that lay behind it.[7]

6. Ibid.
7. Feng, "Mingyun de qushi," 38.

Feng is a gifted raconteur; fiction was thus a natural choice for him. In fact, he began his literary career as an oral storyteller. Every day he would fill his apartment with an audience of friends and relatives; sometimes he even went knocking on doors offering to tell stories. He became famous for his storytelling. To protect himself from political persecution, he invented foreign settings for his tales of the Cultural Revolution, claiming that they were based on old novels or films from abroad. Every time he repeated a story, he would improve and embellish it.

At night when the guests had gone he would lock the door and write his stories down. Aware that he faced possible execution if caught, he hid his manuscripts carefully, burying them under the floorboards or under the bricks in the courtyard, or pasting them together in layers covered with propaganda posters, intending to soak them apart later. But whenever the ideological campaigns of the Cultural Revolution mounted in intensity, no hiding place seemed safe. For a time he stuffed the frame of his bicycle with rolled-up manuscripts. But fear got the better of him, and he would fish the manuscripts out of their hiding places and burn them or flush them down the toilet. Then he began to destroy his stories as soon as he wrote them: he would sit by the stove and write, read and reread what he had written, then throw it into the flames. He has described the anguish he felt:

This was useless labor, a waste of energy. I couldn't publish my stories, nor could I let anyone see them; I

couldn't even keep them, so what use were they?
What a foolish thing to do! How hopeless it was! I
suffered the worst during the clearheaded moments
when I would suddenly deny the value of what I was
doing.[8]

Eventually Feng decided to continue to save his manuscripts despite the danger. But in 1976 his house collapsed
in the Tangshan earthquake; along with his other possessions, his hidden manuscripts were lost. He estimates
that the political and natural disasters between 1966 and
1976 cost him over one hundred manuscripts.

In 1977, after the death of Mao and the fall of the
Gang of Four, Feng's fiction finally began to appear in
print. His first publication, written in conjunction with
Li Dingxing, was the historical novel *The Boxers*, an
outgrowth of his research in local history. The novel
depicts the Boxers as peasant rebels, a "safe" topic according to Communist orthodoxy. Fortunately, literary
controls were soon relaxed enough so that by 1979 he
was able to switch to stories of contemporary life, which
is where his true interest lies:

I don't want to write about these things [historical
topics] anymore. Now, as long as it's permitted, I
want to write about the present. I'll go back to historical fiction if contemporary topics are ever forbidden again. I'm still interested in history, but I just

8. Ibid., 39.

don't have time to work on it now; I'm trying to write as much as I can about contemporary life.[9]

Since 1977 Feng has published two novels (both historical), seven short novels, more than thirty short stories, two screenplays, and numerous essays. His story "Chrysanthemums" won a prize in the 1979 national short story competition; "A Letter" was chosen in the 1977–80 national short novel competition. He is now vice-chairman of the Tianjin branch of the Chinese Writers' Association and a member of the Chinese Artists' Association and of the Society of Folklorists.

Feng is also a critic of contemporary Chinese literature, and his views provide a key to the success of his works. He has published pioneering and controversial essays in which he asserts the primacy of the artistic and humanistic functions of literature over the sociopolitical, a reversal of Maoist orthodoxy:

As I see it, there are six possible vantage points that a writer may adopt: historical, temporal, social, human (*renshengde*), philosophical, and artistic. Among these, we have always slighted the *human* and the *artistic*.[10]

9. Feng Jicai, interview with Margaret Decker, Tianjin, 1982.
10. Feng Jicai, "Xia yibu ta xiang hechu?—gei Liu Xinwu tongzhi de xin" (What is the next step?—a letter to Comrade Liu Xinwu), *Renmin wenxue*, 1981, no. 3: 91.

Feng has even gone so far as to advocate that Chinese writers begin to look beyond the "social problems" of political origin that have preoccupied them since 1977:

> Our generation has written mostly about "social problems." We were driven to do so by the numerous, pressing "social problems" of the times. We yearned to solve them, for everyone to get his share of happiness, and for peace in the world; and we described (or exposed) these "social problems" anxiously, courageously, and passionately.
>
> But if we continue to write like this, we will limit our options; we will end up forcing ourselves to bring up a deep, sensitive, universally significant "social problem" every time we write. The popularity of this method of writing has led to stereotyping and an overemphasis on content in contemporary literature. We young and middle-aged writers have become aware of this recently and have begun to explore our own individual creative approaches.[11]

As an alternative to writing about narrow "social problems," Feng suggests that Chinese writers explore "human life" (*rensheng*),[12] or "human nature":

11. "Yan Wenjing, Feng Jicai tongzhi guanyu chuangzuode tongxin" (Correspondence on literature between Yan Wenjing and Feng Jicai), *Xingang*, 1981, no. 5: 70.
12. Ibid.; and Feng, "Xia yibu ta xiang hechu?" 91. Feng's stance sparked a literary controversy over writing about "social problems" as against writing about "human life."

All writers, Western or Chinese, share certain concerns. There are basic factors in human nature that go beyond cultural differences, or class differences, the feelings of sympathy, pity, or jealousy, for example. All people share these things. At the Yan'an Forum Mao said there were only two different kinds of human nature: that of the proletariat and that of the bourgeoisie. Writers now, at least some of them, have different views. Human beings are complicated creatures. Any given person can be a mixture of selfishness and selflessness, for example, and we cannot say why sometimes he is the one and not the other, why sometimes both, and so on. Some people here, of course, think that the writer should not emphasize the *natural* inclinations of humans, their sexual desires and the like, but that emphasis should be put on the more social inclinations. But, while people exist in a social situation, they exist there in all the complexity of human nature, which, if we are to be realistic, we cannot minimize.[13]

Yet Feng by no means rejects the political function of art; rather, he includes himself in the ranks of writers "who have a strong sense of social commitment."[14] Indeed, his original inspiration was political, and most of his stories have controversial political events or social situations as a backdrop. His works provide ample evidence of an outspokenness that has survived even the

13. Michelson, "Cultural Scars," 13.
14. Feng, "Xia yibu ta xiang hechu?" 90.

ideological clampdown of 1981. (See, for example, the August 1981 story "Winding Brook Way" and the August 1982 story "The Street-Sweeping Show.")

While Feng acknowledges the significance of the literature of social protest that has dominated the Chinese literary scene since 1977, he is highly critical of most of it in artistic terms. He points out that the popularity of most of the recent, daring literary works has been ephemeral because they were "acclaimed for political rather than literary reasons."[15] He calls on Chinese writers to refine their literary technique and on critics to pay attention to technique as well as social content. Writers should stop being intimidated by critics who oppose the concept of art as self-expression, he says, and work to develop their own personal artistic styles. He reminds his contemporaries that the mere reporting of events is not art: if works of literature are to have enduring interest, writers must pay more attention to language, imagery, description, structure, point of view, and characterization.[16]

The latter is a problem about which Feng, in keeping with his resolve to explore human nature, has written at some length. The characters in contemporary stories about social problems, he maintains, are often mere embodiments of abstract social forces rather than believable

15. Feng Jicai, "Zuojia yao ganyu rende linghun" (Writers must delve into the human soul), *Zhongshan*, 1982, no. 5: 111.
16. Feng Jicai, "Xiaoshuo chuangzuode yige xin qingxiang" (A new trend in fiction), *Renmin wenxue*, 1982, no. 8: 111; "Zuojia yao ganyu rende linghun," 112.

human individuals. Such fiction divides people too neatly into heroes and villains according to political criteria and overlooks the complexity of human nature. Moreover, in depicting people as mere pawns of social forces, such stories underestimate the importance of the individual personality. As he points out: "If you put a different protagonist into the same situation, your tragedy might not turn out to be tragic at all. . . ."[17] To Liu Binyan's famous slogan that writers must "delve into life" to expose social ills, Feng adds his own dictum that writers should "delve into the human soul" to create convincing individual characters.[18]

The controls on Chinese literature may be tightened without warning at any time. In the fall of 1983, a campaign was launched to purify Party ranks and to "eradicate spiritual pollution." Yang Hansheng, vice-chairman of the China Federation of Literary and Art Circles, stated this campaign's implications for the arts as follows:

All our literary and art workers should adhere to the slogan of literature and art in the service of the people and of socialism, and to the socialist orientation of literature and art. But some writers and artists have shown themselves apathetic by their manifest lack of interest in writing about revolutionary history or the Four Modernizations; or by their fondness for love

17. Feng, "Xia yibu ta xiang hechu?" 90.
18. Feng, "Zuojia yao ganyu rende linghun," 111–12.

12

stories and the fabrication of bizarre, preposterous plots; or by concentrating on depressing, negative things; or by playing up abstract notions of "the value of the human, humanism, or universal human nature," and calling for a "return of human nature," etc.; or even by writing pornographic descriptions or propagating religion and feudalism.[19]

Yang blamed "weak, lax" leadership for this "spiritual pollution" and proposed that it be "eradicated" through "criticism and self-criticism meetings" for writers.

The campaign seemed to call for an end to the "social problem" literature of recent years, along with the more humanistic brand of writing that Feng Jicai represents. Foreign observers feared for Feng's safety.[20] Now that the campaign has ended, those fears have proved excessive. But the campaign has served as a reminder that these stories were published only by grace of a precarious freedom.

July, 1984

19. *Renmin ribao*, 11 Nov. 1983.
20. *Huaqiao ribao*, 12 June 1984.

The Mao Button

We stand to gain by contemplating recent history while it is still fresh in our minds.
The Author

He vowed to get himself a stupendous Mao button to-night after work.

Actually, the one he had worn to the office today was big and novel enough to arouse a good deal of envy.

His brother-in-law had gotten it specially for him from a certain unit in the navy and had brought it to his place just last night. Everyone in his family had wanted it. After squabbling over it for about half an hour, they had agreed to take turns: each would have it for a day until it had circulated once, then each would keep it for a week at a time. He had gotten it first, not because he was head of the house, but because he had wanted so desperately to show it off at work. He had insisted, and he had won.

He was delighted with himself all morning at the office. He created a real sensation. "You've outdone us all today, Mr. Kong!" said everyone who saw him, as they bent down to pore over the button as if it were some kind of jewel.

Their envious looks went straight to his head. He was certain that his Mao button was the best at the office today. At lunch he paraded around the cafeteria to make sure everyone noticed him. But then Mr. Chen, from the production department, approached him sporting an even bigger, newer, more eye-catching button on his neatly pressed jacket. An embossed portrait of the Leader was centered in a great red enamel sun, below which a giant golden steamship forged through the waves. The Leader was depicted from the front instead of the usual profile. He was wearing an army cap, and his cap and collar bore insignia. The gilding was superb: the flash of gold against red dazzled the eye. The button was a collector's item. Kong felt his own button darken like a light that had gone out. And it was so small by comparison—his whole button was no bigger than the portrait on Mr. Chen's, whose entire button must have been more than three inches across: about as big as a sesame cake.

Mr. Chen was extremely coolheaded and always kept a straight face. As they walked by each other, Mr. Chen just eyed Kong's chest and passed him like some champion athlete meeting a young amateur. Hurt, jealous, and angry, Kong made up his mind to go right out and get an enormous Mao button, even if it cost him his life's savings. He just had to bring Mr. Chen down a peg or two.

When he got home in the evening he told his family

about his failure. After a quick dinner he found all the Mao buttons in the house, wrapped them in a handkerchief, and stuffed them into his pocket. He even snatched up the buttons his wife and son were wearing. Then he dashed out to The East Is Red Avenue, the busiest shopping street in town. He had heard that the open space beyond the parking lot of the big department store was the place to go to trade Mao buttons. People said you could get all the latest styles there. He had never been before.

By the time he got there the sky was dark and all the lights were on, but shoppers still crowded the street. Practically everyone was wearing Mao buttons; they seemed to have become another part of the human body. Some people wore four or five across their chests, the way European generals used to wear their medals a hundred years ago. It seemed to Kong that people with unusual Mao buttons held their heads higher than the rest, while those with ordinary little outmoded buttons moved drearily through the crowd. No matter how much status, income, or power you had, the quality of your Mao button was all-determining at this particular moment. Had the Mao button become the acid test of the wearer's political stance and loyalty to the Leader? A touchstone? A monitor of the heart?

As he walked he paid no attention to the people coming toward him; he had eyes only for their Mao buttons. Colorful, glittering buttons of all sizes were rushing at him like stars shooting by a rocket ship in outer space.

Then he spotted a button exactly like Mr. Chen's. He reached out and grabbed its wearer by the arm.

"Just what do you think you're doing?" the man demanded, obviously startled.

Kong took a closer look at him: a short, fat, paunchy old soldier. Perhaps he was an officer.

"Excuse me, uh—" Kong asked with an ingratiating laugh, "could you spare your Mao button? I have all kinds—you could have your pick. Do you think we could make a deal?"

The soldier sneered as if to say that his button was a priceless family heirloom. He looked annoyed at Kong's effrontery. Kong was still clutching his sleeve. "No way," he snapped, shoving Kong aside, and waddled away.

Kong was angry, but he comforted himself with the thought that even if he had gotten the button, it would merely have put him on an equal footing with Mr. Chen. What he wanted was to outdo him. Then he caught sight of the swarm of button traders beyond the parking lot. His heart began to pound like that of a fisherman who spots a shimmering school of fish, and he broke into a run.

Once in the crowd, Kong felt hot and flushed, but the sight was mind-boggling: an endless variety of Mao buttons and an assortment of hawkers to match.

Some wore the buttons they hoped to trade and called out what kinds they were looking for:

"Who has a Wuhan Steelworks 'two-and-a-half'?"—

a button two-and-a-half inches in diameter—"I'll swap you for it!"

Some displayed their buttons on hand towels; others, who mistook flashy colors for beauty, had their wares in flat glass cases lined with colored paper on the sides and green satin on the bottom. Still others pinned their buttons to their caps so that people had to crane their necks to see them. The crowd thronged the south and east edges of the parking lot. Some people had even spilled over into the lot and squeezed their way in between the cars. With their haggling, shouts, and laughter, the place was noisier than an open-air market at the busiest hour of the morning.

Someone tapped him on the shoulder. "What kind are you looking for?"

The speaker was a big, tall middle-aged man with the unctuous manner of a practiced salesman. But he was wearing a baggy blue jacket with only a single bottlecap-sized Mao button on the chest. He did not look as though he had any special goods.

"I want a big one. At least a 'three-and-a-half.' Do you have any?"

"Oh-ho—no little trinkets for you, eh! Do you mind if the workmanship is a bit rough?" the man asked. He seemed to have what Kong wanted.

"Let me see it."

"First tell me what you have," the man replied without batting an eyelid. He was as haughty as a Mao-button millionaire.

"I've got dozens of different kinds," said Kong, reaching for his pocket.

The man touched Kong's wrist. "Don't take them out in this mob. Somebody'll swipe them. Come with me!"

They elbowed their way out of the crowd, crossed the street, and entered the dark alley beside the Revolution Hat and Shoe Store. The man led him to the second lamppost.

"Let me see your goods," he ordered.

Kong handed the man his handkerchief of Mao buttons. The man inspected them, shaking his head and clucking in disapproval, and gave them back.

"You got any better ones?" he asked after a moment's thought.

"No, these are all I have."

The man paused again. "You're going to have a hard time trading that bunch of buttons for a 'three-and-a-half,'" he said, pointing at Kong's handkerchief of buttons. "Don't forget—the big ones are hot items now."

"Well, I should have a look at yours, whether you're going to trade or not. Then we'll see what's what," Kong retorted scornfully. After all, he had not even seen the man's wares.

Instead of answering, the man unfastened his outer jacket and whisked it open. Kong's eyes nearly popped out of his head: at least a hundred different Mao buttons were pinned to the man's inner jacket. He was a walking Mao-button treasure house. Kong had never seen any of the styles before.

"You haven't seen anything yet," the man said before Kong could look his fill. "Take a peek inside—that's where the big ones are." And he opened the button-covered jacket to reveal yet another garment laden with row upon row of shiny buttons. They were huge: all were at least as big as a fist, and one, the size of the lid of a mug, caught the eye like a crane among chickens.

"That's the one I want!" cried Kong in delight, his heart thumping.

"What? This one?" the man asked with a chuckle. "Do you know how big it is? It's a 'four.' You see where it says 'Loyalty' three times in gold along here? This is a 'Triple Loyalty'[1] button from Xinjiang. Nobody around here has seen these yet. I guess you don't know the market: even four times the buttons you've got here wouldn't buy you one of these. All your buttons put together are worth at most a 'three-and-a-half.' And that's only if you trade with me—nobody else would give you such a good deal. Your buttons are too little and too ordinary."

"Why don't you just let me have this 'four'? I've got forty or fifty buttons here, and—" Kong pleaded. He was madly in love with the button. If only he could just wear it tomorrow, Mr. Chen and everyone else at the office would be green with envy.

Just then a swarthy little man appeared on the left and approached to look at the Mao buttons on the tall man's chest.

The tall man glanced at the newcomer and yanked

his outer jacket shut. "No deal!" he announced rudely, and stalked away, jingling like a horse in bell harness.

Kong thought, "I can't let him get away—at least I've got to trade him for a 'three-and-a-half.'" He was about to run after the tall man when the swarthy little man put out an arm to stop him. With his chin of bristly black stubble and his dark clothes, he looked as if he were carved in jet. His round gleaming eyes seemed to cast a black luster over his entire person.

"Don't trade with him—gypping beginners is his racket," he said in a rasping voice. "Those 'Triple Loyalty' buttons from Xinjiang are a dime a dozen; they're considered passé. Now tell me what you've got—I'll make you a deal. *I've* got a Mao button like nothing you've ever seen before."

"Is it big?"

"Big! Well, it's bigger than that 'Triple Loyalty' button of his. But it's not just big—it's a real novelty. But let me see yours first."

Kong produced his package of buttons again and let the man examine them like a customs inspector. Then the man led him deeper into the alley. The streetlights were burned out, and it was pitch-dark. Kong was afraid that the stranger was going to mug him. The farther they went, the darker it got, until the man's murky silhouette almost blended into the gloomy black shadows.

"Couldn't I take a look at it here?" he asked, making a supreme effort to be brave.

"All right," agreed the swarthy little man, and like the

tall man before him he unfastened his jacket, but his chest was a dark blur without a single Mao button. Before Kong could ask any questions he heard a click, and a round, glowing, moonlike object magically appeared on the man's left breast. It seemed to Kong that a luminous hole had opened up in the man's chest or that his heart had lit up. And inside was a picture: a color portrait of Chairman Mao waving from the Tian Anmen Rostrum!

When he recovered from his momentary stupefaction, Kong understood: the man was wearing a round glass case lit by a flashlight bulb. In the case a color photo of the Leader waving a giant hand was mounted behind a red cardboard railing. The light bulb was probably between the photo and the cardboard. The battery was concealed on the man's person; the wiring hung down from the back of the case; and the switch was in his hand. A flip of the switch and presto! The Mao button would light up like a color television. A truly great invention!

The man clicked the light off. "Well, how do you like it?" came his smug, wheedling voice in the dark. "Isn't it incredible? What'll you give me for it? But don't forget that the batteries and switch alone are worth a lot of money!"

Kong had to agree that the button was a real novelty. But his interest quickly faded. This was some homemade contraption, not a proper button. And you had to carry around a complete set of electrical equipment—wiring, batteries, a switch—as if you were an electric fan. Besides, it might be eye-catching at night, but it would be totally lackluster by day.

"It's very nice," he said politely after a moment's thought, "but I think I won't take it, since it's not a proper button. What I'd like is a regular button, at least a 'three-and-a-half,' if you have any."

The man launched into a sales pitch, but Kong would not change his mind. Then the man grabbed him eagerly by the wrist. Kong, who had been afraid to start with, thought the man was going to rob him of his Mao buttons. Jerking his arm free, he ran for the brightly lit entrance to the alley.

"Stop him!" he heard the man shout behind him.

It occurred to Kong that some of the man's cronies might be lurking nearby. He shot out of the alley and into the street, where he almost collided with an approaching bicycle. Skittish as a hare, he jumped over the front wheel and darted back into the crowd of button traders by the parking lot. For fear that the swarthy little man might spot him, he stooped over, hiding his face, and stole through the crowd. Luckily he escaped without further mishap and ran all the way home.

When his wife saw how pale and breathless he was, she thought he was ill. She scolded him, once she found out what had happened, and poured him a hot cup of tea to calm him down.

"You've got Mao buttons on the brain!" she said. "You never do what you're supposed to when you get home from work—and tonight, of all things, you run out onto the streets to swap buttons. Don't you know what kind of riffraff you could have run into out there? And you took the kid's and my buttons too! If they'd been stolen, what would we have worn tomorrow? People would say I'd gone without my button because I didn't love Chairman Mao. They'd arrest me as a counterrevolutionary, and there wouldn't be anybody here to cook for you when you got home from work every day. It takes finesse to get good Mao buttons. Look at Mr. Wang—now there's a real operator. He may be unassuming, but he's got more buttons than anybody."

"Which Mr. Wang?"

"The one who lives on the third floor of the front building. You still don't know who I mean? Of course you do—Mrs. Wang's husband. What's the matter with you? Did they scare you silly out there?"

"Oh—yes—I see. So where does he get so many buttons?"

"He's on the staff of a badge factory where they make nothing but Mao buttons. His boss gives him hundreds of them to take along on every business trip. You have to grease palms with them nowadays to get a hotel room, buy train tickets, or ask anyone a favor. They're worth more than cash. A little while ago Mrs. Wang told me that her husband paid for a new truck for his factory with nothing but Mao buttons."

"How many buttons did that cost?"

"The man's clever—he may not have parted with all that many. My guess is that a shrewd fellow like him lines his own pocket on the sly whenever he has the chance. Why else would Mrs. Wang have a new Mao button every time I see her? When I ask her about them she just laughs it off instead of answering, but I'm sure she gets them all from her husband. Just now I went over there to collect their water bill[2] and found them gloating over their buttons. I burst in without knocking and really got an eyeful."

"Did you get a good look at them? What kinds did they have?"

"I couldn't begin to tell you. There were at least a thousand—the bed and table were both covered with them."

"Were there any big ones?"

"Big ones? I swear one of them was as big as a saucepan lid."

So the object of his far-flung search had been right next door all along. Leaving his tea untouched on the table, he ran to the front building as fast as his legs could carry him. "Mr. Wang!" he began to shout, even before he got to the third floor. Like some invisible hand, joy clutched at his vocal cords and made his voice tremble.

Once inside Mr. Wang's apartment, he begged him to show his treasures. Mr. Wang grudgingly obliged, since Kong was an old neighbor. Now here was a great Mao-button collection! Mr. Wang was a Mao-button millionaire if there ever was one. Kong was developing an inferiority complex.

Then he spotted the enormous button that his wife had mentioned. Mr. Wang said that it was a "five-and-a-half." Kong weighed it in his palm. It was surprisingly heavy: at least half a pound. But the picture was commonplace: a big red sun with a profile of the Leader in the middle and a chain of nine sunflowers across the bottom. The flowers looked more like coarse sieves. The buffing, painting, and gilding were shoddy. However, it was definitely the biggest in the world—Mr. Chen's would look tiny by comparison. Kong wanted a big one: they were the best—they stood out and really made a statement. He begged Mr. Wang for it and showed his buttons one more time. Luckily he had one with a picture of the globe and the caption: "The People of the World Yearn for the Red Sun." Mr. Wang happened to need this one to complete a set of four, so Kong gave it to him, along with two others, in exchange for the biggest button in history. He arrived home cradling his treasure in trembling hands.

"Wow!" his wife and son exclaimed when they saw it.

The next morning he rose early, shaved, washed his face and neck, and put on clean clothes, as carefully as if he were going to be awarded a medal. Next, ignoring his wife's protests, he used one of her soft new handkerchiefs to polish the huge button with petroleum jelly. He had some trouble pinning it on. It covered half of his narrow chest when he wore it on the side, but placed in the middle it looked frivolous, like the breastplate of an ancient general. And his jacket sagged under its tremendous weight. Worst of all, since the pin was right in the center of the back, the button tilted outward like a picture frame instead of lying flat. Kong was at a loss until his wife suggested that he change into his denim jacket; although the weather was still too warm for denim, the stiff material allowed the button to lie flat the way it was supposed to.

With the button on, he struck a few poses and admired himself in the mirror.

"Hooray!" his son cheered, clapping his hands. "My dad is tops! My dad is number one!"

The child was adorable—his compliments were the icing on the cake.

Yes, he really was the sensation of the day! People ogled him as he rode his bicycle down the street. Some pointed him out to their companions, but he sped past them before they could get a good look at him. He was on cloud nine. To prolong the gratification, he took the long way to work. People on a passing bus pressed their noses flat against the windows to stare. As he approached the gate of his office building he tensed up like an actor about to take his first plunge through a brightly lit stage door. He was headed for the limelight.

He entered the gate and locked his bicycle in the yard.

"Hey, everybody," someone shouted, "come see Mr. Kong's Mao button!" In no time flat he was surrounded by a crowd. People were jostling each other and craning their necks to see. They were looking at his button with amazement and envy, and at him with a new respect. Everyone was yelling, which attracted more people.

"Now that's a big button. Where did you get it?"

"Mr. Kong, you're a real go-getter!"

"Of course! I'm loyal to Chairman Mao," he said with

a smug laugh, keeping one hand on the button in case anyone tried to snatch it.

Some people tried to move his fingers out of the way so that they could get a better look at the button; others tried to peek at the back to find out where it was made.

"It doesn't say anything on the back," he cried, clutching the button. "It was produced by a classified military factory. Please quit yanking on it, the pin is too small—" He seemed anxious, but in fact he was jubilant. The excitement he was causing was a sign that his button was without compare not only at the office, but probably in the whole city. Unless someone made a button as big as a crock lid, which only a giant could wear. Then he remembered Mr. Chen: where was yesterday's victor now?

The crowd had swelled to thirty or forty people. Everyone was babbling at once. He could not hear anything. His heavy denim jacket had brought the sweat out on his forehead. Unable to stand it any longer, he began to wriggle his way out of the unbearable crush, away from the hands that were pulling on him.

"Let me out, you're squashing me!"

He was tickled pink.

Finally he squeezed his way out like a noodle out of a noodle machine. He was exhilarated. But just then he heard a clank, as though a heavy metal platter had fallen to the ground. Then he heard it rolling around. He did not realize what the sound was until he reached up and found that his Mao button was gone.

"Oh, no! My button fell off!" he cried. Everyone

froze and he began a frantic search. It was not on the ground in front of him, so he stepped back to turn around and look behind him. He felt something hard and slippery underfoot.

"Oh, no! You're standing on a button with a portrait of Chairman Mao!" he heard a woman say, before he could grasp what had happened.

In terror he looked down and saw the Mao button under his heel. He should have been able to lift his foot quickly, but it was as unresponsive as a piece of wood. His body went limp and his weight sank into the offending leg. With all eyes riveted upon him, he stood rooted to the spot.

This blunder was a heinous crime that brought him to the brink of destruction. There is no need to recount the details here. Suffice it to say that he recovered from his Mao-button mania and came to look upon these former objects of his affection with fear and trembling. These events are all behind him now. But there is one question that puzzles him to this day. Perhaps the only clue to its answer lies in the following "natural phenomenon": you can travel the entire three million seven hundred and seven thousand square miles of our country today and see hardly a single Mao button. . . .

Chrysanthemums

He was dazzled by the gorgeous phoenix-tail chrysanthemums.

From a high trellis they cascaded to the ground in a shower of shimmering flecks of light, as if they were a magnificent phoenix tail, or a long sequined skirt spotlighted on a stage, or a silent, fragrant waterfall. The long, blossom-laden stems fell loose and free, like a girl's freshly washed hair; they hung in tangled profusion and breathed a wild, woodland scent. The phoenix-tail chrysanthemum was his favorite flower, the only one that attained such marvelous perfection.

Transported by the beauty of nature, he slipped his hand mechanically into his pocket, took out a big carved walnut pipe, put it to his mouth, and lit it. As soon as he had taken a few puffs he realized that smoking was prohibited in the greenhouse. Nervously he looked around for a place to put out the pipe and glanced over his shoulder to make sure that the custodian had not spotted him. Fortunately, all was still and there was no one in sight. But just as he breathed his sigh of relief, he noticed the weathered face of an old man peering at him from behind a nearby clump of huge green canna leaves. The face was shockingly grotesque. He figured this must be the custodian and wondered how long he had been hiding in the leaves watching him. The old man's small gray eyes were fixed on the fuming pipe. But to his surprise the old man waved to him before he could apologize for his transgression.

"It's all right," he said amiably. "Come with me."

Astonished, he followed the old man through the canna leaves to a corner of the greenhouse.

Along one wall there was a brick *kang*[1] with a mat and a bedroll on it. Beside the *kang* lay a heap of gardening tools: short-handled hoes, long-handled clippers, sprayers, buckets, twine, and bamboo rods. In the middle of the clean, damp earthen floor stood a foot-high square wooden table that looked as if it belonged on the *kang*, along with two tiny chairs like the ones used in kindergartens. The unvarnished legs of the furniture were stained halfway up with water from the floor. On the table was an old newspaper covered with drying tobacco leaves. He realized that the old man must be the gardener. He vaguely remembered the fellow from the few times that he had been there before, but this was the first time that he had ever really noticed him.

"Go ahead and smoke. There's good ventilation here," the old gardener said, pointing to a small open window over the bed. Then he invited him to sit down and poured him a cup of heated water, even setting it respectfully before him. The offender wondered uneasily what he had done to deserve such treatment.

The old gardener sat down opposite him and took out a long-stemmed pipe and a round shiny tin-plated tobacco case. Then he opened the case and started to fill the pipe, but his hands trembled so much that he was not very efficient. Once he had lit the pipe and started to smoke, he remained silent but kept smiling at his companion while casting sidelong glances at the pipe in his mouth. It was impossible to divine what thoughts were concealed by the gardener's grotesque features. Was this his good-natured way of mocking him for his error? Or was he trying to show goodwill?

"Mr. Tang, are you still painting these days?" The old gardener broke the ice.

"How do you know my name is Tang? And that I paint?" he asked, taken aback.

"What?" The old gardener cocked his right ear.

He repeated in a louder voice.

"Of course I know," the old gardener answered with a genial smile, the laugh lines on his cheeks crinkling into symmetrical curves. "You once brought your students here to sketch the flowers. You haven't changed a bit."

After a moment's thought Mr. Tang remembered: Before the onslaught of the Cultural Revolution in the mid-1960s, he had brought his art class here when his favorite phoenix-tail chrysanthemums were in bloom. The old gardener had not forgotten, though six or seven years had gone by. The abrupt twists and turns of recent years had pushed the past so far out of his own mind that it all seemed like ancient history.

He had been a celebrated painter but had fallen into disgrace, like a glittering chandelier that had been knocked down, smashed into rainbow smithereens, and trampled callously underfoot. The world had forgotten him. In better days visitors had flocked to his house, but now "his gates were deserted and few carriages came to call."[2] All the people who had pestered him before—celebrities, honored guests, reporters, editors, disciples, admirers, and idle hangers-on—had disappeared without a trace. He was as useless as a postmarked stamp. But now to his surprise he found that he had been inscribed in this old man's memory. He could not check the wave of grief and tenderness that welled up inside him.

"I'm surprised you remember me. What a good memory you have. But I—uh—don't paint much anymore." His voice faltered with emotion.

"What?" The old gardener cocked his right ear again.

"I don't paint much anymore!"

"I see." The old gardener nodded sympathetically, like a close friend. "But you ought to paint, you know," he added emphatically. "Your paintings are beautiful, really beautiful!"

"They are? But you've never seen them." He knew that he had never painted when he had taught his art class here. Suddenly he suspected the old gardener was toadying.

"Yes, I have," said the old gardener. "There are prints of your paintings. I've seen them. They're really beautiful!"

The old gardener's praise sounded heartfelt, as if he were recalling the flavor of a particularly tasty fish. Apparently the old man had paid some attention to his works and knew of his reputation. Could it be that an appreciative friend was hidden here in this colorful world of exotic flowers and plants, like a Zhong Ziqi in a secluded mountain valley?[3] He looked in amazement at the old gardener, but a couple of searching glances at his grotesque features was enough to put such odd conjectures to rest.

Who could find a trace of intelligence, beauty, or knowledge in this ugly old gardener? His black jacket and pants were wrinkled, dirty, and worn to a shine at the elbows and knees. He was wearing padded cotton shoes and the puttees of a peasant. Where shadows fell on his swarthy face it was as black as the bottom of a frying pan, blending with the black of his outfit just as his wrinkles matched the creases in his clothes. He was short and squat, with a slight hunchback and pronounced bowlegs. Hunched over, he was like a big black earthenware pot from the Han dynasty—one of those curious utensils that came only from the marvelous imaginations of those first-century sculptors. A goose egg bulged on his forehead; his brow jutted out like a primeval apeman's. His eyebrows were thin, his eyes small and redrimmed, and his pupils bore the dull, bleared gaze of old age. Stubble covered his cheeks and chin. His jug ears looked artificial and seemed to strain to catch every sound; his right ear, which was always cocked, appeared bigger than the left.

One sensed that this was an old man who was prejudiced and set in his ways. Like an old mountaineer who had spent most of his life in some ravine, he was uneducated, probably incapable of even writing his own name. He had gone deaf in his old age, and his movements were slow and clumsy. He spilled half his tobacco when he stuffed his pipe, but did not bother to pick up the droppings until he had spilled a great deal. And he did not seem to mind reaching down with a leathery, stubby, rough hand to scoop up a mixture of tobacco and dirt to tamp into his pipe. He spoke little, probably because of his poor command of language. When he praised Mr. Tang's paintings it appeared that the only words at his disposal were "Beautiful, really beautiful!"

In Mr. Tang's experience, people almost never said a painting was "beautiful." The word was profound and seemed particularly incongruous on the lips of this weather-beaten old man. What was he talking about? What did he mean by "Beautiful, really beautiful!"? Could such a word be a heartfelt response to his art? Maybe word of his fame and some prints of his works had struck the old man's fancy, Mr. Tang thought. But the old man's inclination was merely intuitive; it was by no means an appreciation of his art. The old gardener was right, but he was misinterpreting art, just as when we think the twittering of birds is melodious without having the slightest idea of what they are really communicating. We always assume that birds are warbling affectionately to each other or singing a duet, when they may very well be arguing.

They sat for a while. The old gardener seemed to have nothing more to say and enjoyed his pipe in silence; the brass mouthpiece never left his lips. Although Mr. Tang had also run out of small talk, he had at least recovered from his embarrassment and was enjoying his pipe. But for some reason the old gardener kept glancing at it.

"Do you want to try my tobacco?" he asked.

"No," the old gardener answered with a smile that was both genial and repulsive. "I was just thinking— I've never seen a pipe quite like yours before."

Mr. Tang's pipe was unusually large, with a carving in relief of a plump owl perched on a thick, bare branch, and a big full moon—actually just a large circle, but a very neat one—incised into the background to provide contrast to the portion in relief. The design was unique. He emptied the pipe and handed it to the old gardener.

"I carved it myself," he said.

The old gardener took the pipe and began to examine it in fascination.

"It's beautiful, beautiful, really beautiful!" he repeated, looking up at Mr. Tang with sincere admiration in his bleary little eyes. Mr. Tang was deeply moved. The pipe was his pride and joy. But he was firmly convinced that its intriguing formal variations and subtlety of line were lost on the old gardener. He was struck with an unkind suspicion: maybe the old gardener was being so deferential and complimentary because he had taken a liking to the pipe and wanted it for himself.

"If you like it, you can have it," he said, noting that the old gardener seemed unwilling to let the pipe out of his grasp.

To his surprise this brought the old gardener up short. With a grave expression he hurriedly held the pipe out to Mr. Tang.

"No, I couldn't," he said.

"Take it and enjoy it. I have more at home."

"They belong to you. I can't accept such a gift."

The old gardener stubbornly shook his head. Mr. Tang politely insisted but only succeeded in upsetting him. His chin trembled and his features contorted as if he could not bear being suspected of coveting someone else's possessions. He jumped up and thrust the pipe into Mr. Tang's hands. Mr. Tang had no choice but to take it, refill it, put it back to his lips, and light it.

Mr. Tang's understanding of the outlandish old gardener had deepened: he saw him as both obstinate and sincere. The gardener's respect for him was genuine, untainted by any desire for personal gain. But he was still convinced that the gardener was an ignorant man with no more than a layman's appreciation of art. They could never share a common language. Still, he had had his fill of prejudice, indifference, and ostracism, and he prized the respect shown him here. The old man's pure, natural kindness was as rare as flowers blooming after a prairie fire, or green leaves after the first storms of winter.

From then on he often went to visit the old gardener, even though the greenhouse was a good distance from his home. He especially liked to go when the phoenix-tail chrysanthemums were in bloom. After viewing the flowers, he and the gardener would sit puffing on their pipes over two cups of steaming hot water. A colorful sea of flowers surrounded them and enveloped them in its tranquil perfume. There was not a breath of wind, but now and then they got a whiff of peony or a hint of the delicate fragrance of orchid. They would speak very little, often sitting quietly until dusk, when it grew dark inside the greenhouse before the light had faded outside the window. Then all he could see was the blur of colors around him and the murky silhouette of the man who sat facing him. At such moments the old gardener, whose grotesque features were only faintly visible in the flickering light of his pipe, was completely trans-formed into a Han earthenware pot.

From a few idle exchanges of conversation he learned that the old gardener was named Fan and was from Fengrun County, north of Tangshan. He came from a long line of gardeners. He had worked at this little suburban commune greenhouse since he was in his early thirties. He supplied color for meetings of all city orga-nizations and added beauty to the lives of many families. His wife had died of an illness long ago. He had one son, a pump repairman on a neighboring farm. This sunny little greenhouse, with its moist, earthy, scent-laden air, was his home and his entire world. The old gardener apparently had nothing more to tell him.

The two would sit facing each other in silence, without embarrassment at the lack of conversation. On the contrary, each took a sort of satisfaction in the other. Mr. Tang could not tell what it was that gave the old gardener such satisfaction, but the smile in the old man's eyes as he gazed at him and his pipe gave him the distinct feeling—could it really be that this inarticulate old gardener understood his art? No, never. No one could ever imagine the place that this carved pipe occupied in his life and in the realm of his spirit.

Hunger and the need to buy art supplies once drove penniless Parisian artists to paint golden moons on barroom walls in exchange for wine, pickles, bread, and canvas. Then they would hurry home to get their beautiful ideas onto canvas before the food in their stomachs had digested.

Not so with our Mr. Tang. At that time all artists were in a state of enforced idleness. Forbidden even to teach, they just languished at home. On the fifteenth of each month Mr. Tang could go to the payroll office of the Art Institute to pick up his ample salary. Every day he could stuff his stomach until it bulged, but he had no outlet for his energy, and time hung heavy on his hands. Although he felt the constant itch to paint, he did not dare touch a brush.

His was the common plight of all our writers and

artists. A net of electrified wire had been cast over the world of letters, and the garden of painting was littered with mines. Both paintbrush and pen were as dangerous as the trigger of a bomb: one false move could be fatal.

Eventually his tubes of viscous paints hardened into powdery lumps like dead locusts in an entomologist's specimen case; a heavy layer of dust coated his canvases; and shiny cobwebs gathered among the paintbrushes in his brush holder.

He was utterly bored. He had nothing to do all day and seldom had visitors anymore. He cherished his memories of all that he had lost, especially the gratifying limelight of his meteoric rise to fame. In those days good things had come as a matter of course, while his only companion now was loneliness.

But he could not go on living in the past; he had to find some release. He had tried to while away his time by learning to fish and to play chess and cards, but he had found that he lacked patience and the knack of quantitative reasoning and abstract perception. No matter how hard he worked at it, he simply could not cultivate these hobbies.

He had even tried carpentry. He was in fine shape for his fifty-odd years; there was enough strength left in his sturdy frame to handle a big saw or plane. Since a great deal of his furniture had been confiscated during the turmoil of a few years ago, he started to make some useful pieces and found the task quite enjoyable. He laboriously taught himself how to make a rough table or a cupboard, but he was unable to put the finish-

ing touches on anything. He would lose interest in a
piece before it was done, complete it carelessly, and slap
on the varnish. There was always an odd drawer handle
or glass cabinet door that he neglected to install. The
unfinished pieces stood all around his room. Unable to
paint, he was like a jilted lover who cannot summon
the energy for anything.

One day as he sat smoking idly, the big, round, smooth
dark red pipe in his mouth happened to catch his eye.
Suddenly the grain of the wood reminded him of a
couple of the winged celestial beings from the Dunhuang frescoes.[4] In a flash of inspiration he found an
engraving tool and carved along the grain of the wood,
then he gilded the lines he had engraved. The effect was
surprisingly good. The flying angels, with their billow-
ing sleeves and floating, swirling sashes, seemed to soar
slowly through outer space, sparkling in the light of
the sun. Looking at them was as wonderful as gazing
up at the ceiling of the Mogao Caves. The incised lines
had taken on a powerful, distinctive charm that was
entirely new to him. An ordinary, everyday pipe had
been transformed into a splendid work of art, and he
had discovered a whole new universe, an oasis in the
parched desert of his intolerable confinement. Like a
child whose imagination is inspired by a simple wooden
wheel, he began to dabble delightedly with his play-
thing.

He crawled under the bed and found some old pipes
in a tattered basket. Within a few days he had carved
them all. On some he carved great fleets of sailing ships,

and on others, lifelike, downy chirping sparrows. Still others showed water rippling in the spring wind and a few fading stars, or imitations of Han designs of covered war chariots, each line accurately re-creating the archaic flavor of the ancient rubbings.

When he had carved all the pipes he possessed, he made his own out of hardwood, dried brierroot, or ox-horn. His carving grew increasingly skillful. He mastered incising, bas-relief, and high relief; he drilled holes or carved filigree; he learned to tint, polish, wax, and lacquer. His pipes were incomparable: they were far superior to those of ordinary craftsmen, whose glib technique produced only stereotyped clichés. Strictly speaking, their products were mere toys rather than works of art; but no two of Mr. Tang's pipes were alike in modeling, line, imagery, construction, or style. He regarded each of his pipes as a creation and devoted himself painstakingly to each. On every one of these inch-high cylinders he strove for a certain emotional appeal, a kind of perfection.

He filled a glass bookcase with the pipes he had carved —the books had all been confiscated, so it was empty anyway—and they were a dazzling array of superb art treasures. Here were bizarre human forms from the ancient bronzes; pure, lively decorations from the "painted pottery" culture;[5] Roman architecture; the *Mona Lisa*; samurai from the Japanese Ukiyo-e prints; Buddhas from the Northern Wei dynasty; the six steeds from the tomb of Emperor Taizong;[6] the Arc de Triomphe; stone engravings from the Wu Family Shrines;[7]

the horses of Han Gan;[8] the oxen of Han Huang;[9] the bamboos of Zheng Banqiao;[10] the Egyptian Sphinx—even Walt Disney cartoon characters.

Each one was true to the original, preserving its artistic style and appeal. Some of the originals were executed on a grand scale, yet they had lost none of their spirit, momentum, or resonance when carved in miniature on pipes. Some he had fashioned out of gnarled old roots, letting the natural shapes guide his carving of jagged mountains, ancient wine vessels, the heads of wild beasts, the waves of the sea, or drifting clouds.

He chose as his subjects the treasures of the civilized world and the infinite variety of human life. His forms were bold and novel. He preferred to capture the spirit of things rather than their precise outlines. He had always rejected the simple transcription of the images received by the retina. He believed, rather, that the images must be blended on his palette with the tones of his innermost feelings. Now he had completely realized his artistic ideals.

Sometimes he was absorbed in his work all day long, just as he had been when creating a painting. If inspiration came in the middle of the night, he could not resist the urge to jump out of bed and pick up his engraving tool. When he was pleased with his efforts he would even wake up his wife to admire them with him. She had been in his graduating class at art school thirty years before, and her ideals and talents were similar to his. After marriage, however, she had renounced her ambitions for his sake, or rather, she had made his goals her own. Her fragile shoulders had borne the heavy burdens of life, but she had taken pleasure in his success and silently shared the rewards of his career. She had shown less overt concern than he at the announcement of his ruin, although secretly she had been more discouraged than he. Now she was greatly comforted to see that he had found some spiritual solace during his protracted misery. Pipes would always pass unnoticed as toys. A painter was safe as long as he refrained from painting. Sometimes she could not hold back her tears when she saw how much pleasure he derived from these small objects.

Mr. Tang concluded that the old gardener could not possibly understand any of this. He was probably just deluding himself to imagine that the gardener truly appreciated his art. But an artist needs public acclaim, not just the esteem of his family. Perhaps it was that Mr. Tang could not bear being enveloped in silence, and the solitary, hoarse response of the old gardener partly filled the void.

The autumn winds brought a dappling of purple and gold to the uniform greenery of nature. Beauty returned to the world, and chrysanthemums were in season again. But Mr. Tang did not go to the distant little greenhouse; he had not been there for over half a year.

Six months before, the Party had given famous painters back their laurels. He began to have visitors again, just as a branch that flowers after a blight attracts hordes of bees, butterflies, and small insects. Editors came for contributions, and reporters for interviews. His house was host to a continual parade of celebrities. The students who had vanished a few years before returned to ask advice, and there was no end to the number of people who wanted his paintings. He was kept busy all day long just ushering people in and out the door. Sometimes they would come in a swarm, packing his studio until it bustled like a newly opened little restaurant.

He could not get any work done with all these people pestering him. Some dropped in just to pass the time and then would stay for hours; the only reason they left at all was that they got tired of sitting. These tactless visitors had him at his wits' end. Sometimes he deliberately refrained from speaking, hoping his indifference would drive them out, but they were oblivious to his signals. Some of them even asked: "How can you find time to paint with so many visitors here? Can't you stop being nice to them?" The way they always excepted themselves was ludicrous and exasperating.

Nonetheless, he was gratified to have so many people clustered around him like stars around the moon; it was tangible proof of his fame and worth. His lost prestige had returned like an escaped bird that comes home to roost, filling the air with its songs. Dimples of joy played upon his cheeks from morning to night; the procession of visitors pleased and honored him. He was so busy that the insignificant old gardener faded from his memory.

He did, however, continue to make his carved pipes,

because all his visitors asked for them once they found that they could not have paintings. Very few of the people who wanted his pipes really understood the marvelous language embedded in each of these tiny objects, nor did they necessarily like them terribly much (though they pretended to treasure them). They asked for them only because they were carved by the celebrated Mr. Tang, just as autograph hunters ask a great author for a signed copy of his book without intending to read it. Still, he had to comply with their wishes. In the short space of a few months people had taken most of the pipes in his glass case, and he had to find the time to turn out new ones. He carved them hastily and less conscientiously than before, but people still vied for them. He was meticulous about the design or technique only if he was making a pipe for an art expert or some VIP.

He was allowed to paint again but could not for lack of time. For the moment his pipes were more famous than his paintings; he was fast becoming the recognized master in the art of pipe carving.

One day he found his house filled from early morning with illustrious friends. One of them was a short, fat, famous writer who knew something about painting. Two others, who were the same height as each other, both wore round glasses and looked much alike (although one had a long face and the other a small one), were senior editors who had come to press him for contributions. A fourth guest was tall, thin, and long-legged like a stork; he was a painter. They were discussing Mr. Tang's artistic style, for which they naturally, since he was present, had nothing but the highest praise. The long-legged painter, one of Mr. Tang's former colleagues, had not graced his door for many years. Recently he had begun to visit again and had adopted the pose of being one of Mr. Tang's closest and most appreciative friends.

Although Mr. Tang enjoyed listening to them, he wanted to paint and hoped that they would not stay too long. He had made a sketch the night before, intending to complete it that day, but visitors had been arriving continuously since morning, and he felt obliged to entertain them. They had already polished off an entire pack of filter cigarettes, filling the studio with heavy smoke, and still they showed no sign of leaving. He was close to the end of his tether, when there was another knock at the door.

Here comes someone else. I guess I'll just have to write today off as a total loss, he thought in frustration, and went to answer the door.

But his eyes lit up in surprise when he opened it, for he was greeted by a huge pot of splendid phoenix-tail chrysanthemums, held in the arms of someone whose face was hidden by the blossoms. He was stunned. Who would bring him flowers? And such gorgeous ones at that!

"Who is it? Please come right in!"

The visitor plodded in silently, set the flowers on the

floor, and straightened up. Then Mr. Tang recognized the old gardener. He had delivered Mr. Tang's favorite flowers right to his door.

"Oh, it's you, Lao Fan![11] How did you get here with those? Did you carry them here all the way from your greenhouse?"

The stocky old gardener stood smiling affably in his mud-spattered jacket. The long trip had exhausted him; perspiration glistened on his brow, and he was breathing so hard that all he could do was nod his head wordlessly.

The guests rose and gathered around to admire the pot of chrysanthemums.

Mr. Tang invited the old gardener to sit down and catch his breath. The gardener turned to sit in an armchair but then hesitated as if afraid his clothes were too dirty. Spotting a little wooden stool in front of the bookcase in the corner, he went over and sat on that. Mr. Tang did not urge him to move to the armchair.

"How are you? Busy?" he asked, pouring the old gardener a cup of heated water.

"What?" The old gardener still had that habit of cocking his right ear.

"I said, are you busy?" Mr. Tang repeated in a louder voice.

"Oh, no, not really. You haven't been to the greenhouse in six months. The phoenix-tail chrysanthemums are your favorites, aren't they? I figured you'd miss them if you stayed away much longer, so I took off work today to bring you some. Now you can enjoy them at home." As the old gardener spoke he took out his long-stemmed pipe and round tin-plated tobacco case, opened the case, and set it on the ground. He filled the pipe, lit it, and began to smoke.

The guests had returned to their seats, and Mr. Tang went back to his big leather easy chair to resume the conversation. No one took any further notice of the weather-beaten old man in the corner who had brought the flowers. Mr. Tang did not try to make conversation with him either. Instead, he left the gardener to smoke and sip his water alone, though he did smile and nod in his direction from time to time.

Far from resenting Mr. Tang and his guests for ignoring him, the old gardener listened with relish to their rambling conversation. He had cocked his right ear to hear more clearly. His face would furrow with incomprehension, then relax as if he had grasped some subtle point. He sat there quietly, looking quite content, just as when he had sat across from Mr. Tang in the greenhouse puffing silently on his pipe.

Then, discovering the fantastic array of carved pipes in the glass bookcase behind him, he stood up and examined them at length. Awestruck, he pressed himself against the glass doors as if trying to squeeze inside. His hot breath clouded the glass, which he kept wiping with his hand.

"Beautiful, beautiful, really beautiful!" He could not help breathing his peculiar sighs of appreciation.

The guests found such sounds jarring: what an absurd figure this foolish, ugly old man was. Mr. Tang was embarrassed at having such an ignorant, eccentric acquaintance and was afraid to speak to him for fear he might cause him to say anything even more humiliating. He did his best to divert the attention of his distinguished guests from the old gardener and prayed that he would take his leave soon.

Everyone ignored the old gardener. After a while he rose and said goodbye to Mr. Tang, who made a show of good manners and escorted him out the front door.

"I'm afraid I interrupted your conversation," the old gardener apologized.

"Not at all. Thank you for coming so far to bring me flowers," he answered politely.

"Why haven't you been to the greenhouse? All the phoenix-tail chrysanthemums are blooming beautifully this year. You must be busy."

It occurred to Mr. Tang that unless he said he was busy the old gardener might drop in whenever he had the chance.

"I'm more than busy—I'm swamped. These people have nothing better to do with their time than drop in on me, so I never have a minute to myself. And they want my paintings, but when am I supposed to paint? I've only painted four pictures in the last six months, and most of those were done late at night. If this goes on much longer, I'll have to become a hermit in the mountains if I want to get anything done!" His face showed mingled pleasure and annoyance.

"Oh, that's terrible. You ought to paint, you know." The old gardener seemed more worried than Mr. Tang. "Why don't you come and paint at my greenhouse?" he added earnestly after a moment's thought.

"No—I can't get away from here. Sometimes the people who come to see me have real business. Don't worry about me. I'll figure something out."

The old gardener was speechless for a moment. "Well," he said, "I'll be going now. You still have company." And he turned and trudged away.

The old gardener delivered flowers twice thereafter. Both times he placed them quietly by the door and left without showing his face or knocking. Discovering them as he escorted guests out the door, Mr. Tang was touched by the gardener's kindness and meant to visit him, but then it slipped his mind.

Once, when he was opening the window to clear the room of smoke after seeing guests out, he heard someone outside set something down with a clank. He ran to the door and found another pot of beautiful flowers on his step. He caught sight of the silhouette of a stocky old man in black and recognized the gardener by his slightly hunched back and waddling gait.

"Lao Fan!" he called out, running after him. He invited the gardener in.

"No thanks. Don't waste your time," the gardener said, shaking his head.

"There's no one here now. Why don't you come in for a moment and catch your breath before you go back?"

"No, thanks. This is your chance to do some painting. I'm not tired. I'll be home before I know it."

"Don't come so far out of your way anymore after this. This pot must weigh a good ten pounds. I'll go to the greenhouse if I want to see the flowers," said Mr. Tang.

"You don't have time," said the old gardener. He could not forget how Mr. Tang had complained of the lack of time to work.

"But—you haven't even asked me to pay for them. I can't let you deliver flowers for nothing."

"Don't mention it," said the old gardener, shaking his head. "I only have one son, and he supports himself, so he doesn't cost me anything. I have more money than I need—I don't drink and have nothing to spend it on. I even grow my own tobacco. Please don't mention money."

"But how can I thank you?"

"What?"

"I said, I should thank you somehow."

"Do you really want to thank me?" The old gardener's bleary little eyes peered out in astonishment from beneath his bronzed, protruding brow.

"Yes."

"Well—" The old gardener hesitated for a moment, then continued decisively, "I'd like to have one of your carved pipes then." His expression was one of earnest entreaty, but he also looked embarrassed, even ashamed, to be making such a request.

"What? All right! That's easy enough. I'll go inside

and get one for you." Mr. Tang turned and went into the house, thinking that the old gardener was terribly eccentric. He had offered him a pipe on the first day they had met. Why hadn't he taken it then?

Mr. Tang opened the glass doors of his case. There were not many pipes left. On the top shelf only five remained, of which two were masterpieces that he had been reluctant to give away. The other three, recent creations, were exquisite too, but they were spoken for. They had been made to order for a famous poet, the chief of the Municipal Art Bureau, and a great movie director. Each was fine enough to be in a museum. Without touching them, he chose a pipe adorned with five rather simply carved peonies from an assortment of ordinary pipes on a lower shelf. It was an amateurish effort, one of his earliest pieces, but he figured that it was good enough for the ignorant old gardener. Polishing the pipe in his palms, he took it outside.

At the sight of the pipe the old gardener's eyes twinkled like little gray light bulbs, surprising Mr. Tang with their expressiveness.

"Do you"—the old gardener's voice quavered with delight—"really want to give me such a fine pipe?"

"Of course, take it!" Mr. Tang said, handing it to him. He took satisfaction in the old gardener's obvious pleasure: at last he had repaid him for delivering the flowers.

"Thank you, Mr. Tang, thank you very much. I'll be going now—" the old gardener stammered gratefully, taking the pipe solemnly in both hands.

He turned and walked away, his eyes glued to the pipe cradled in his palms.

Mr. Tang sat in his leather easy chair puffing on his pipe. He was slumped so low that the chair seemed about to swallow him up. He looked as if he had plopped down there in exhaustion after three days of continuous hard labor.

His eyes were bleary and listless; his cheery dimples were gone; and his shoulders were hunched up as if to ward off the cold—although it was only early autumn and he was wearing two heavy sweaters. Total silence reigned in the room, and dust coated the furniture, which had not been polished in several days. There had been no visitors.

One of his paintings had inexplicably been deemed counterrevolutionary by the same Municipal Art Bureau chief who had commissioned one of his carved pipes. Although this bureau chief personally rather liked his paintings, he had blotted him out in order to toe some preposterous line handed down from above, and climb another rung on the ladder of power. After enduring repeated political attacks, Mr. Tang had been cast aside to await his fate.

All was lost again. He found himself ignored once more. Now, as before, only he and his wife crossed his threshold. The babble of voices had vanished from his studio, leaving it as hushed as a small restaurant in the wee hours of the night. But a few pipes commissioned by famous and important people still lay on the top shelf of his glass case. Exquisite as they were, no one came to claim them.

Strange to say, he found seclusion a welcome change. He had learned to deal both passively and actively when confronted with life's ups and downs. At any rate, he no longer regarded his fleeting glory—the illusory feeling of being a moon surrounded by stars—as the most precious thing in the world.

There was a knock at his door, a sound he had not heard in a long time. Putting down his pipe, he shuffled across the room to see who it was.

He raised his eyebrows in surprise at the sight that greeted him: in his doorway stood a man bearing a pot of giant golden phoenix-tail chrysanthemums. The long stems trailed clear to the ground, although the bearer of the flowers was holding the pot in front of his face.

It was the old gardener—Lao Fan! Of course it was he. He might keep his distance when times were good, but he always turned up at moments like this. He had always been an undemanding, sincere friend. To Mr. Tang the heady aroma of the flowers seemed blended with pure human kindness. He was dumbstruck.

"Come on in, Lao Fan—come right in—all right— just put them on the floor. They're beautiful! What a big pot! It must be terribly heavy."

The visitor put the flowers down and straightened up. When he got a look at him, however, Mr. Tang was startled to see that it was not Lao Fan, but a stranger: a young man of medium height wearing a black cotton jacket. He looked like a peasant, with large hands, a broad chin, small drooping eyes, coarse weathered skin, and mud-spattered shoes.

"Who are you?"

"I am the son of your acquaintance Lao Fan."

Mr. Tang recognized the family resemblance. Quickly he invited him to sit down and poured him some hot tea.

"How's your father? I've been meaning to go see him." Mr. Tang spoke in earnest; he was not just being polite.

"My father got caught in the rain last summer and died of pneumonia," the young man answered unexpectedly. His voice was subdued, yet he showed no sign of violent grief, as if he were speaking of the distant past.

"What? He's dead?"

"As my father lay ill on the *kang* he kept telling me that these were your favorite flowers, Mr. Tang. He was growing this pot of them specially for you. He said that I should be sure to deliver them if he was gone by the time they bloomed."

Mr. Tang was astounded. A man he had not considered worthy of his esteem had treated him with respect and sincerity. Sadness came over him; he was at a loss for words. Mechanically he picked up his pipe from an end table, but his hands were trembling so much that he could not strike a match.

"Mr. Tang," said the young man, as if the sight of the pipe had reminded him of something, "do you know how much my father loved your carved pipes? You once gave him one, didn't you? Well, as he lay dying he said to me, 'Remember, I don't care what kind of clothes you bury me in when I'm gone, but you musn't forget to put the pipe Mr. Tang gave me into my mouth.'"

"What?" Mr. Tang cried in shock, as if he had not heard clearly, when he had in fact heard perfectly.

The young man repeated himself, but Mr. Tang could not hear a word for the buzzing in his ears.

To this day Mr. Tang often recalls the old gardener's hoarse, foolish sigh of appreciation: "Beautiful, really beautiful!" Then he wonders: Could the old gardener, who raised so many exotic flowers with his own coarse hands, really have been ignorant of beauty? In his mind's eye the weather-beaten old man is no longer grotesque but has been transformed into a beautiful, unforgettable soul. At such moments guilt weighs on his heart like a heavy slab of stone. He wishes that he had given the old gardener his most exquisite pipe when he had the chance. . . .

Numbskull

"Oh, what a numbskull I am!" I tell myself, rapping my knuckles on my empty head.

I'm an impractical egghead, with none of the savvy it takes to get along in the real world. My wife doesn't beat around the bush—she just calls me "Numbskull." At first she only resorted to such an insult when she was furious at me for botching something important. And did it ever burn me up. But I got used to it after a while. My two little sons would even chime in with it from the sidelines whenever my wife was bawling me out. "Numbskull" became my family's nickname for me. And now I even use the name myself when my own bungling gets me down.

Because of me, our whole family has to crowd into a dingy little ten-by-ten room. Pushy neighbors have partitioned off the hallway and left us only a tiny patch of territory by the door for our small coal stove. All

our worldly possessions are crammed into our room.
The only spot we can find for our entire winter's supply
of cabbages is under the bed. The room smells so bad
I have to leave the door open when I get home from
work or when we're going to have company. You'd
probably choke if you dropped in unexpectedly. And
there isn't even standing room for guests, so whenever
anyone comes over I hurry around the room taking
the washbasins off the chairs and hiding them under
the table, moving the stools, pots, and pitchers from
the middle of the floor to the nook by the bed, and
hustling the kids off to sleep. I get even more nervous
when the guests are my wife's friends, because then
she'll nag me mercilessly right in front of them and
glare at me as if to say, "Look what you've reduced me
to, you bungling numbskull!"

I'm just as unhappy as she is. I'm a technician at the
Radio Institute, and I always bring my work home from
the office. After my wife and kids have gone to bed I
clear away some of the crockery on the little table,
spread out my blueprints, and work late into the night.
I drape the light bulb with a sheet of black paper so as
not to disturb my wife's sleep. I don't even smoke cigarettes, because striking matches makes too much noise.
If I thoughtlessly rustle a paper or two, she'll let out a
groan to signal me that I'm getting on her nerves. Then
the only way to avoid a tiff is to put my things away
and climb into bed. But first I have to tickle the kids'
feet so they'll give me back my territory, which they

always invade in the abandon of sleep. And I don't dare get up to go to the bathroom, because I know the others will have stretched out into my space before I get back.

Living like this has caused any number of spats between me and my wife. In the beginning our love was as poetic and picturesque as a clear, sparkling stream, but now the stream's been dammed up with the pebbles of reality. The strong affection of our courtship days has gradually paled into indifference. She's just not what she used to be. According to her, my honest kindliness is stupid bungling, my devotion to work is selfishness, and I care for myself to the exclusion of my family. We quarrel about these issues. I fly off the handle and throw things to bully her, while she cries and hollers to make me give in and apologize. All of which gets us nowhere.

I used to think these arguments were just an unavoidable, harmless part of being married. I had no idea how bad things were until one day when she suddenly announced she wanted to leave me. After that I started to do my best to let her have her way and to keep my mouth shut when she nattered at me the way women will. But a dreadful rift had already opened between us, there was no denying it. After giving the matter careful thought, I finally identified the root of our misery: our housing problem. It could spell domestic tragedy unless I confronted it squarely. I made up my mind that at least half the energy I usually devoted to my work would have to go toward getting a new apartment.

A rare smile flitted over my wife's dried-up, sallow face when I told her. Then she scoffed, "This is the first time you've ever volunteered to do anything you're supposed to do—but I'll bet you're the kind of—"

I was sure she was going to say "numbskull," but she didn't—I guess she was trying to encourage my first effort to please her.

"—person who'll botch it," she concluded, changing her tack.

"No, I'm not!" I insisted, partly to spur myself on and partly to reassure her.

I wrote an application describing all the pressing reasons why I needed to move, made several copies, and took it to the Housing Authority and to my boss. I went with a chip on my shoulder, as if I thought they owed me something and I wasn't going to take no for an answer. But they just refused me flat out or passed the buck in a polite, friendly sort of way.

"Feng," my boss said to me with a genial smile, "we've known about your troubles all along, without your even telling us. But with housing as tight as it is these days, what are we supposed to do? We can't exactly clear out an office for you to live in. Besides, there are eleven young people in our institute waiting for living quarters so that they can get married. Some of them have been waiting for three years. If we had any housing to give out, who do you think would deserve it most?"

My cheeks burned with shame. I felt unreasonable, like a troublemaker.

My wife blew her top when I told her, however. She hauled out the nickname "Numbskull," which she'd kept in reserve from before. "I'll give you three more months to do something about this," she threatened me, "or else we'll have to split up. I'll take one of the kids with me to my parents' house!"

I was at my wits' end until my colleagues told me about a new trick: apartment trading. With all the millions of families in this world, I figured, somebody must want a smaller apartment. What if some of the occupants of a large apartment had moved out or the rent was too high? I knew it was a long shot, but I figured I might as well try my luck. So I set to work making 250 "Apartment for Trade" notices and stayed up till dawn plastering them around town. I covered all the busy intersections, big hotels, bus stops, movie theater bulletin boards, and hospital waiting rooms.

Within three days I'd gotten results beyond my wildest dreams. A steady stream of people came knocking at my door: men and women, old and young, short and tall, fat and thin, from all walks of life, and with all kinds of faces, personalities, clothes, and accents. I spent my evenings receiving them, negotiating with them, and ushering them in and out, sometimes until ten at night. And on Sundays I had to go see their apartments.

I'm the kind of guy who almost never goes visiting. I found out how many different types of houses there are in the world. Some families were even worse off than we were. I visited one place where seven or eight people

from three generations were crowded into a squalid little room even smaller than ours. In the middle they had
built a loft, where all four children were perched. When
I arrived a row of small, nearly identical heads poked
out and eyed me quizzically, like baby birds in the eaves
of a house.

After more than two months of fruitless searching I
began to realize that everybody who wanted to trade
apartments was after the same thing I was: a few extra
yards of space. And I was worn out. My old stomach
trouble was back because apartment hunters were interrupting my dinner night after night. My cheeks had
collapsed like deflated rubber balls. My heart wasn't in
my work. I kept asking for leave to go see apartments,
which put me in the bosses' bad books. The disapproval
I detected in their eyes was quite unnerving. And as
for my wife, she was fed up with all the tiresome, useless hostessing. Her eyes had dark rings under them,
like a panda's, and she looked as withered and dispirited
as leaves after an autumn frost. The funny thing was,
she didn't bawl me out or yammer at me the way she
used to. She hardly said anything but just went on
patiently building her castles in the air.

One evening someone came to look at our place. Before I had a chance to find out what he wanted, he
pointed at our room, gave it the thumbs-down, and
walked out shaking his head.

"That does it!" said my wife. "We'd better forget
about this trade idea or it'll be the death of us!"

Fortunately she didn't start fuming at me again about

a separation. But I was still worried. I rushed out and raced around town for another whole night tearing down my "Apartment for Trade" notices.

When my colleague Chen—who was in charge of the maintenance and food service—heard about what I was doing, he said, "You'd better quit advertising so indiscriminately or criminals posing as apartment traders will come to case the joint. Then one day while you're out they'll jimmy your lock and make off with everything. Why don't you let me introduce you to a fellow I know, Feng. He used to be my neighbor. All he had when he started out was a bathroom. He's moved fourteen times in five years. He buys nothing but portable folding furniture so he won't be tied down. In his latest move he organized an eight-family trade-off and got himself a new apartment while he was at it. It's a big, sunny second-story suite, and it has four thirteen-by-thirteen rooms."

"How did he swing that?" I exclaimed. "Somebody else had to lose out so he could get an extra apartment— why did they let him get away with it?"

"I just told you—he engineered an eight-family trade-off. These deals are his specialty. The biggest one he ever managed involved eleven families. When a lot of people exchange at once, some will be trying to get nearer to their workplaces and others will be looking for cheaper rent or a nicer place. So he always manages to finagle an apartment for himself in the shuffle. Boy, does that guy have get-up-and-go! He's a night watchman at the rubber factory warehouse, which isn't exactly a restful job. He spends all his days looking at housing, and he knows every building in the city like the back of his hand: what it looks like, its layout, its facilities, how many apartments it has, how big each one is, and which direction it faces. He's really more professional than those cadres over at the Housing Authority who just sit around and stuff their faces all day. He knows all the right people and can get things done. He's a great talker too. Do you think it's easy to get eleven families to move at once? He had to talk them all into it. I'm a neighbor of his from way back, and I'm on pretty good terms with him. Once I helped him get the angle irons he needed to make a bed. I'll go see him tonight and have him come over to your place tomorrow evening. I'm sure he'll be able to help you. What do you say?"

"Wonderful!" I was so delighted, I felt like kow-towing to Chen. "I'll be waiting for him at home tomorrow night at eight. What's his name?"

The name he gave me was quite a surprise. It had an intriguing ring to it: "King of the Movers."

The next evening my wife and I eagerly awaited the arrival of our "little savior." We straightened up the room, polished the little table, set out fancy cigarettes and fruit, made a pot of our best tea, and put the kids to bed. The King of the Movers turned up on the dot of eight. He was short, skinny, and pimply. He impressed me from the start as capable and experienced. He stuck out his right hand and shook with us briskly, diplomat style, while his wide, shrewd eyes shone into my face like twin flashlights.

"I'm Liu Baoliang," he said, and sat down. My wife quickly got out a cigarette and handed it to him. He grabbed it, stuck it into his mouth, lit it, took a couple of puffs, and sized up the room. "There are four apartments in this building," he observed, "two facing east, two facing west, and one bathroom, right?"

My wife and I were taken aback. "How did you know?" I couldn't help asking.

He chuckled instead of answering. He looked like a real expert. My wife and I exchanged joyful glances: now that we had met this fellow, there was hope for us yet!

"I hear you specialize in radios," he said, taking another drag from his cigarette and breathing out clouds of smoke.

"Yes, I do."

"Know how to fix them?" he asked with interest.

"Well, mostly I just design circuits," I answered.

His look of interest vanished, and he exhaled the rest of the smoke in his mouth. "Why don't you learn how to repair them? Now, that's a useful skill!"

My wife shot me a withering glance, as if reproaching me for my obtuseness. "He can do most ordinary repair jobs," she chimed in. "Is your radio broken? Feel free to bring it on over. The guys at the Radio Institute are all experts."

"That's right." I caught on to what she was up to and

hastily tried to remedy the situation. "I can fix them. If you need anything, just let me know!"

"No, no. I don't need anything; I was just asking." He gave a satisfied chuckle and waved the hand that held his cigarette. "Can you fix TVs?"

"Yes, sure I can," I replied eagerly. As a matter of fact, I didn't know the first thing about fixing TVs.

The King of the Movers eyed me with exceptional interest and goodwill. Next, with a birdlike movement of his head, he turned to my wife. "And where do you work?"

"No. 4 Hospital."

"Are you a doctor or a nurse?" he pursued, quickly raising his eyelids with their dense growth of matted lashes as if he had caught a glimpse of a profit.

"I'm at the registration desk. If there's ever anything I can do for you, just come on over!" said my wife, glancing at me to make sure I noticed the example she was setting.

The King laughed, and his gaunt features crinkled in a little wave of merriment, then subsided into a most peculiar expression. I couldn't tell if it was derision or pity—it was totally baffling. But then he told us in no uncertain terms what he had in mind.

"Mr. Feng, I can see at a glance that you're an honest guy. You want to know how I can tell? Look, you fix radios and TVs, and your wife works in a hospital. That's enough to have gotten you out of this shabby little hole ages ago. Now, I don't like to beat around the bush, and besides, we're hardly total strangers. After all, Chen introduced us. If you'll excuse me for coming right out with it—seems to me you just haven't got any finesse."

"That's right! That's just what I'm always telling him, but he won't admit it." My wife looked as if she'd finally found herself a powerful ally. Now she had someone to support her standard gripes about me. I was afraid she'd get carried away and call me "Numbskull" in front of a stranger. But mercifully she just remarked, "Feng is such a stick-in-the-mud. We really need your help."

The King had smoked his cigarette so quickly that it had already burned almost all the way down to his fingers. Helping himself to another from the pack on the table, he lit it with the butt of the first one and turned to me with a smile.

"Don't be such a stick-in-the-mud, Mr. Feng," he admonished me, "or you'll never get anywhere in this world. Loosen up a little and learn to turn things to your own advantage. If I was as smart as you and could fix radios and TVs and things—and I'm not just boasting, either—why, by now I'd have myself one of those nice little foreign-built houses. What's the matter, you think I'm vulgar? Well, maybe I am, but I've got what it takes. I'm not educated like you—but I'm certainly better off than you! I can get all the things you can't. I'm a thoroughly practical man. I say people have an instinctive drive to eat and dress well. Can you sit there and tell me you don't have such a drive? I certainly can't claim to be above such things. But so what? I would never deprive myself by living in a little hole like this. No offense—I'm just telling you this for your own good. You're probably going to say that you're doing it for some 'cause' or for your 'work.' But who's going to look out for your interests? The good things in life aren't going to deliver themselves to your doorstep. Take apartments, for example. I'll bet you submitted an application to your bosses, and I can guess what they said—that there's a housing shortage, so it's no dice, right? What a lot of malarkey! It's just because you're a nobody; if you were the secretary of the Municipal Party Committee you could get a great big suite without even lifting a finger. But if ordinary folks like us want to live better we've got to rely on ourselves, on our own know-how and finesse. What do you say, am I right?"

I must admit I found his theory convincing. There was nothing I could say against it. I felt as though he'd wised me up and I was about to turn over a new leaf. But I still drew a blank when I thought about the concrete problem of getting an apartment. "Finesse? Finesse—but—"

Without making the slightest effort to be polite, he threw me a mocking look with his big, shrewd eyes. That was probably all a bungling numbskull like me deserved from a man of such infinite sagacity. Next he asked my wife for paper and pencil and scribbled out a sloppy, misspelled list of names and addresses. "Go check out all these places," he said, handing it to me.

"We'll take it from there." He rose, shook hands with me briskly, and took his leave. My wife and I saw him to the front door. I was still clutching the promising scrap of paper covered with his dense, blotchy scrawl. We bowed and thanked him repeatedly.

"Don't mention it!" he said with a wave of his hand. He was holding a cigarette that he had lit on his way out the door. "To tell you the truth, I don't want anything from you. I'm only helping you out because you're such babes in the woods. I'll be back in a few days. See you!"

Before going inside, we waited until his silhouette had vanished into the night. Great benefactors like that don't grow on trees, I thought to myself.

I took the next day off from work and made a tour of the apartments on the King's list. Every one of them was nicer, roomier, and sunnier than mine. To think that such places were within my reach! I was practically bursting with joy. Like an old peasant in a parched field longing for rain, I began to yearn for the return of the King of the Movers.

Three days later he turned up, radiating the good cheer befitting a savior, even though he was tired and sweaty from lugging a huge TV. I informed him that all the apartments on his list were eminently satisfactory, and that if I could just move into any one of them I'd consider myself in heaven and wouldn't presume to make any further worldly demands. Patting me on the chest, he told me he'd do his utmost and urged me to bear with him. Next he asked me to fix the TV set he had brought.

Naturally I was eager to do a favor for someone who was so willing to help me. However, I knew nothing about fixing televisions. So I took it to work the next day and had an expert do the job for me. He changed two tubes, but I never dreamed of asking the King for the money. And thus began the close association between this extraordinary personage and myself.

He came almost every day to discuss trading my tiny abode for one of those lovely palaces. He filled me with hopes, promises, and strategies. Patient planning, he taught me, was the only way to win. He was about to orchestrate an unprecedented fifteen-family grand trade-off. This was the only solution to my problem: he would subtract a bit from each of the fifteen households and end up with something for me. But they would all have to enter gladly into the trade-off, and that would depend upon his own know-how, persuasive powers, time, and energy, so the feat would involve considerable personal sacrifice on his part. His worldly experience and determination boosted my confidence.

In the meantime he had me repair all sorts of radios, televisions, hearing aids, irons, electric fans, and blow-dryers, saying that they belonged to his close friends and relatives. To show him I understood the sort of back scratching that's so common these days, I took all these objects with me to work without the slightest hesitation and asked my colleagues to repair them. He also kept my wife busy finding doctors, arranging for hospitalizations, and buying costly drugs, even plasma, for his friends and relatives. Once he paid us three frantic visits in the course of a single week. He was in desperate need of some medicine or other. I thought someone in his family must be at death's door.

At first we didn't mind running these errands. After all, we were grateful to him. But when his promises didn't come true and his charm started to wear thin, my wife began to suspect that he was just using the apartment as bait. I thought it was unfair of her to attribute such base motives to our warmhearted benefactor, and this led to a quarrel. But by the time I'd cooled off, I found myself agreeing with her. Still, I just couldn't get rid of him. Every time I tried to refuse one of his requests, he would talk me into sticking with him. He began to remind me vaguely of a leech.

One night after dinner he arrived with a twenty-inch color television for me to repair. My wife showed absolutely no sign of enthusiasm or welcome. She didn't even look up from the sweater she was knitting for one of the kids. "Mr. Liu," she said jokingly, but in a voice edged with scorn, "it's high time we got some results from you. We're about to turn into a TV repair shop here!"

I was afraid the King would be offended, but he didn't seem to mind at all. Far from looking displeased, he burst out laughing. "Feng is going to have to lend me a hand with this TV here. As for the apartment—well, you picked the right time to ask. I'll be able to get you one very soon. But you're going to have to grit your teeth and give a little 'blood'!"

We were flabbergasted. Was he just dangling fresh

bait? Or was it true? And he was being so cryptic. When I asked him to explain, he began by scolding us laughingly. We were being downright unfriendly, he said. Here he had run his legs off to find us an apartment and we were worse than ungrateful. Why, we had even taken him to task! The reason we'd had to wait so long, he explained, was that nobody wanted my little apartment. But then he added that he would soon be able to get us a new one-bedroom apartment.

"But you're going to have to come up with one of these," he continued, pursing his lips in the direction of the television on the table.

"You mean give somebody a big color TV?" My heart leaped into my throat.

"No, no," he scoffed. "Take it easy! It doesn't have to be this big. A twelve-inch black-and-white will do the trick. It'll cost you—" bending his thumb down, he stuck out four stubby fingers at us.

"Four hundred bucks?"[1] I had recovered from the initial shock, but it had occurred to me that this was exactly the sum total in our bankbook.

"You think that's too much? Hah! Feng, if I stood out on the street and hollered, 'I've got a new apartment here for the first person who gives me four hundred bucks,' I guarantee you a crowd would gather in no time flat and practically eat me alive. For four hundred bucks all you can get is a bathroom. Why don't you go out and ask around, find out what things cost these days. People will spend a thousand bucks to get their sons transferred back to the city from the countryside!"

He had misunderstood me—as a matter of fact, I was terribly excited by his news. My wife kept her head, however.

"Just where is this apartment going to come from?" she inquired, shooting me a silencing glance.

The King of the Movers paused mysteriously for a moment. "I'll let you in on the secret," he told us sternly. "But whether the deal goes through or not, you'd better keep mum about it. The apartment is going to come from the Municipal Department of Housing Distribution. Who else has new houses? The four hundred bucks isn't for me, it's for somebody over there. I'm doing all this legwork for you out of the goodness of my heart."

"Do you mean that *we* can get an apartment from the city?" I asked.

"Come on, Feng, get with it! The apartment is his to give out, after all. Don't you realize that he can give it to anyone he wants to? I can see that the fine points of all this are lost on you."

"But can he accept a TV from us? Wouldn't he get into trouble if anyone found out?" I continued, like a stupid pupil questioning a learned teacher.

At this the King burst into peals of laughter, as if to remind me what a foolish, ignorant egghead I was.

"Why would I waste my breath telling you all this if he couldn't accept it? If you give him a TV, he'll give you an apartment. As for how he's going to do that, that's his problem. And as far as the TV goes, if you don't let the cat out of the bag, nobody's going to ask you about it. But in case anybody ever does, just say you lent it to him, and you'll be off the hook. You get it? It's foolproof!"

I did get it, and I smiled. Boy, these guys really know what they're doing, I thought.

I have to hand it to my wife that she stayed cool at such a moment. "Mr. Liu," she asked, "do you think we can count on this? Is this guy really all that powerful?"

The King of the Movers hesitated a moment. "You'd better not breathe a word of this to anybody," he whispered. "Here's the lowdown: he's the chief of the Bureau of Housing Distribution! All right? He's got the keys to all the new apartments in his pocket. If you'll just shell out a little, I guarantee you'll be able to get an apartment right away. You can have your pick of the new ones on Red Flag Street. And let me give you one more tip: the TV is a wedding present for his son. He doesn't need a thing himself. He already has a twenty-four-inch Japanese color TV. You won't get another chance like this in a million years! Don't shilly-shally or somebody else will beat you to the punch. Oh, and you're to buy him the TV—no cash. In deals like this, cash is taboo."

"But where can we get a TV? They're in such short supply!"

He pointed to the huge television he had placed on our table. "I can swing that if you'll fix this one. It belongs to my brother-in-law, who's an accountant in the wholesale appliances section of a department store. I'm sure he can get us one."

It dawned on me that the King of the Movers got a kickback with every move he made.

My wife and I sat there basking in contentment. After nearly twenty years of marriage, the bird of good luck had finally perched on my shoulder. Perhaps all was not lost.

"When do we start, Mr. Liu?" my wife asked, jubilant but still wary.

At that, the King jumped up and took me by the arm. "Let's go, Feng. What do you say we go to Chief Li's house right now?"

"What? Oh! All right!" I sprang to my feet, adding, "I'll take this TV of yours to work tomorrow. I guarantee it'll be fixed in three days."

His eyes brightened. "That's more like it, Feng!" he exclaimed.

As he praised me I caught a glimpse of my wife. She was eyeing me with rare appreciation. I swelled with pride: I had climbed a rung on the ladder of life. For once the wheels had started to turn inside my thick skull, and all of a sudden I was savvy. I resolved to pull off this deal with the influential Chief Li. My new finesse would bring me happiness. Once and for all I was going to shed the stigma of the nickname "Numbskull."

Chief Li's house was dazzling. Five spacious rooms, bright lights, snow-white walls, sofas, armchairs, floor lamps, television set, electric fan, tape player, etc.—a complete collection of all the latest status symbols. Colorful gilt, glass, and plastic glittered and sparkled on every side. I felt as if I'd stumbled into the Crystal Palace of the Dragon King. Most of the furnishings were so modern they hadn't even come on the market yet. The place looked like the home of a couple of newlyweds, but as a matter of fact, Chief Li's sons were well beyond childhood. They were elegantly dressed. The youngest was kicking a big orange ball back and forth from one room to the other. I thought how my own sons played Ping-Pong on the bed. If their ball rolled onto the floor, it was gone forever—vanished into a pile of junk. If only we could live like this!

Chief Li was nothing like what I'd imagined. I'd been expecting a jowly, paunchy, senior type. He was only in his early forties, however, and had a pale, sickly, stony face. His inky black hair hung like crow's wings from his center part. Looking utterly jaded and humorless, he slouched silently in his handsome armchair. With his index finger he kept scratching the side of his right nostril, which looked slightly inflamed. Unnerved by his manner, we didn't know how to begin—especially since he didn't even bother to look at me or ask my name. For him I didn't exist.

Fortunately the King of the Movers had a smooth tongue in his head. He made small talk with the chief about various people and things, mostly who it was that could help you buy this or take care of that problem, and so on. Boastfully, he tried to tempt the chief with news of all the latest bargains he had heard of. He was a little obsequious, I thought.

Chief Li listened halfheartedly, studiously avoiding the King's gaze. Every once in a while he would ask a perfunctory question.

"What kind of shoes? Where do you get them?"

"At the Foreign Trade Office. They're letting them go for half price, but they're top quality. High-grade leather, soft as satin. It's a rare opportunity, and they're going like hotcakes. But I'm sure I can get you some if you want them. I'm on great terms with Vice-Director Xu over there. Last month when his wife was sick I got him medicine three times in one week, all special imported stuff that you just can't find anywhere in stores."

I remembered how the King had asked my wife to get him medicine. So that was what he'd been up to.

"Then bring me a sample pair," commanded Chief Li coldly.

"Be glad to. Just leave it to me. If you want, I can get you a whole crate."

I noticed how Chief Li dwarfed the superhuman King of the Movers, making him look like an errand boy or a broker who runs his legs off for a commission. Chief Li, on the other hand, was a big boss who had money and power at his disposal. All state welfare had to pass through the hands of men like him. He was a fat-cat philanthropist. Most people who sought him out were trying to sponge on him. No wonder he gave everybody the cold-shoulder treatment. Power was the quickest route to arrogance, wasn't it? Even if he received me in his underpants, I wouldn't dare complain, since he was the one with the apartments. The space I needed for survival was his to hand out. He had all the advantages. I made up my mind to clinch the deal.

The King had steered the conversation around to me. "This is Feng from the Radio Institute. He's been wanting to come see you for a long time. He knows all about TVs. If anything goes wrong with yours, feel free to call on him."

At this, Chief Li glanced up for the first time and gave me the once-over, but casually, and still without addressing me. I saw my time had come. I steeled myself and tried to look shrewd.

"If there's anything you need, Chief Li," I said, grinning from ear to ear, "just let me know. I hear you want a little TV. Well, I happen to have just bought one. It's brand-new, and it's just sitting there at home with no one watching it. If you'd like, Chief—" I cut myself off abruptly. The King was anxiously frowning at me to shut up. His eyes seemed to be saying that I'd gotten us into real hot water.

Bewildered, I was casting around for something to say next when Chief Li rose and told me huffily, "I don't need a TV." Then he turned to the King with a grimace and said, "You'd better go home now. I have to go down to city hall for a meeting in a little while." Going to the door of one of the adjoining rooms, he called his son, a droopy-eyed, chubby boy, and asked him to show us out. The boy's manner was stiff, probably the effect of having such a powerful man for a father. As soon as we had gone out he slammed the door shut.

Once outside, the King let me have it. I was rude, rash, stupid, and gauche. "Feng," he cried, "how could you say such a thing? You can't talk about these deals openly. He's a real big shot! Did you think he was going to show his hand to you? And now you've gone and betrayed me. He won't trust me anymore. He's sure to think I spill the beans to strangers. How am I supposed to keep on dealing with him after this? You've gone and cut off one of my contacts, that's what you've done!"

I begged his forgiveness, pleading that I was ignorant and had never learned to weigh my words properly. But he just said, "Forget it!" and stalked away.

I'd never dreamed that such a man of the world could be so hot-tempered. I couldn't bring myself to tell my wife what had happened. But the next day at the office the King called to say that he had gone back to Chief Li's house the same night, explained to him that I was his cousin, not a stranger, and promised that I wouldn't get him into trouble. He had had to lay it on thick to get us out of the mess I had made. And Chief Li, after careful consideration, had finally agreed to let me trade a television for an apartment. Within three days I was to have the King deliver the TV to Chief Li, who would not see me again. The King was to act as go-between in all transactions. I would have to wait until the following month for the apartment. Chief Li had given his word that the deal would not fall through.

While I had the King on the phone I apologized and thanked him, my voice trembling with joy. When I got home from work I told my wife about the phone call, making a clean breast of my bungling the day before. She bawled me out and told me to get to the bank on the double. But just as I was leaving she stopped me.

"We haven't known the King of the Movers long," she said uneasily. "We don't know much about him, and we haven't gotten a thing out of him in the few months since we met him. He's just been using us. Do you think he's on the level? Besides, Chief Li said yesterday that he didn't need a TV. How come he needs one now all of a sudden?" She paused for a moment, then continued, "And now he says Chief Li won't see you anymore, and that he'll take care of everything. Maybe he's trying to trick us. These are our life's savings. If we get gypped, we'll have nowhere to turn. We'll be ruined, and we'll just have to grin and bear it. Leave the money in the bank until you see Chief Li and get the word from the horse's mouth." And she took the bankbook out of my hand.

The King called me daily from then on to urge me to hurry up and get the cash. He said he'd found the TV for me, and that all I had to do was pay for it and it would be mine. The more he pressed me, the more we figured he was up to no good, and the tighter we held on to our money. One day I told him I wouldn't shell out for the TV unless I could see Chief Li again. He lost his temper and started to yell at me over the telephone. "All right! So you don't trust me! Here I am trying to help you, and you treat me like dirt. You think I'm trying to bleed you? Well, I wash my hands of the whole business!" Like a housefly, he buzzed off. And that was the last we heard from him.

The loss of the King of the Movers put an end to our only hope, faint as it had been. I was afraid my wife would start bickering with me again. Funny thing was, she didn't. But for a long time she seemed pretty glum.

One evening after dinner more than two months later, there was a knock at the door. I answered it. In the gloom of the unlit hallway I saw a pale, stony face. I recognized the visitor by the cold glint in his eyes.

"Oh, Chief Li! What are you doing here? Come on in!"

This man had the power to bestow happiness on millions of families. I would never have dreamed that he would seek me out. Why had he come? I invited him in repeatedly, but he refused.

"If you've got a minute, why don't you come for a walk with me," he suggested dryly.

"All right!" I was so keen on buttering him up that I didn't take the time to go in and tell my wife. I just shut the door and went with him.

He was really an oddball. Offering no explanation of why he had come or where we were going, he walked the whole way in silence. As for me, I'd learned my lesson the last time. I was afraid to open my big mouth again. All kinds of questions were on the tip of my tongue, but I vaguely sensed that something good was in store. Was he taking me to fix a TV, I wondered. If he could use me, nothing bad could come of it.

We walked quite a distance. Ahead of us in the night loomed the murky outline of a huge complex of buildings dotted with a few lighted windows. I now saw that we had arrived at the new housing project on Red Flag Street.

He led me to an entry in the middle of the second row of buildings, and we went inside, groping our way to the second floor in the dark. Taking a key from his pocket, he inserted it in a lock, turned it with a crunch, opened the door, and flipped a switch, flooding a brand-new one-bedroom apartment with light. The walls were a dazzling white. The air had that delightful new-house aroma of fresh plaster and paint.

Without waiting for me to catch on, he asked casually, "Will this do?"

I got butterflies in my stomach. Was this apartment for me? I couldn't believe my ears. Stupefied by such a sudden stroke of good luck, I almost hugged the eccentric, baffling bureau chief. "For me? This apartment? Why? How can it be?" I cried.

Without answering, he left me standing foolishly where I was and took a couple of turns around the empty adjoining room. Then he came back and said, "I had to call your office to get your address. I need to ask you a favor."

"What is it?" I asked eagerly. My tone of voice implied, "For you, I'd even go pluck the stars from the sky."

"I need four hundred dollars in a hurry. I'm wondering if you can get it to me first thing tomorrow morning. As for the apartment—nothing to it. I'll do my best to get it for you. But you'll have to wait till it goes through central distribution. It'll probably take me about six weeks to get you your Notice of Housing Allotment."

"That's wonderful! The money's no problem. I'll get it first thing tomorrow and bring it over to your place."

"Don't bother bringing it over. I'll be at your door tomorrow morning at ten. And there's one more thing we've got to get straight—I'm not going to give you an IOU. I'll pay you back within three months. You trust me, don't you?"

"Of course! Don't worry about paying me back. Just take the money!" I was bursting with joy and gratitude, but I was so awkward, I couldn't think of anything nice to say.

He gave me a stern warning not to breathe a word of the matter to the King of the Movers. Then we left the building and went our separate ways.

I couldn't wait to tell my wife the good news. On the way home I tripped over a stone on the ground. Never had I been so agile—like an athlete, I just bounced right up again. When my wife heard the whole miraculous story, she had me take her to the darkened housing project to see the door of the apartment that would soon be ours. Next we looked around for a while in front of the housing project. We didn't get home until eleven. Neither of us slept a wink that night.

In the morning I got the cash. At ten sharp, at my

door, I handed it to Chief Li. He took it and left without a word of thanks. I found his behavior reassuring: he wouldn't have been so rude and matter-of-fact unless he meant to get me that apartment.

That was the beginning of a period of domestic bliss. For the first time in years my wife's easy smile returned. Her nerve-racking carping stopped. And she was patient with the children. Best of all, she quit scolding me and interfering with my nighttime work. She was even understanding. If only we could live like that forever! My inner happiness pepped me up at work. I amazed my bosses. They had no idea how much energy a little hope can give.

After a couple of months I still hadn't gotten the keys or the Notice of Housing Allotment from Chief Li. For fear of pestering him and botching the whole thing, I refrained from going to see him. When I couldn't stand it any longer I would go and look at the apartment on Red Flag Street to see whether anyone had moved in. The windows were always dark. They seemed to be saying, "There is still hope. Be patient."

Two more months passed and winter set in. One night after dinner there was a knock at the door. I opened it and in came a boy I didn't recognize. He was chubby, with drooping eyelids. I had the feeling I'd seen him somewhere before, but I couldn't quite place him. He pulled a thick package from his breast pocket and handed it to me. "My father wants you to take this and give me a receipt," he said stiffly.

It was Chief Li's son. I grabbed the package and tore it open: a wad of one-dollar bills. What was it for? Was he paying me back? I riffled through the bills. There was no note, nor was there the Notice of Housing Allotment I'd been waiting for so anxiously. Foreboding gripped me. I turned to my wife. Her eyes mirrored mine, and they were wide with bewilderment.

"Uh—is that all your father said?" I asked the boy eagerly.

He was as cold as his father. "My father says to tell you he's working on your problem," he answered. "He says arrangements like this are not easy to make these days and wants you to bear with him. He also says you should count the money while I'm here."

When I heard this I knew all was lost. This wad of bills had been tied to that apartment the way a string tethers a bird. The string had been returned to me, but the bird was gone. My head was reeling. I was crushed. I wanted to stuff my life's savings back into the boy's pocket, even though I knew it would do no good.

He was getting edgy. "Come on, count the money and make out a receipt," he said. "My mother's taking us to the movies tonight."

I didn't have the heart to count the money, so I just scribbled out a receipt for him. I couldn't help adding a pitiful plea: "When you get home ask your father whether my apartment—"

"I've got nothing to do with it. You'd better ask him yourself," he interrupted harshly. And taking his receipt, he left.

It was a staggering blow. We were dumbstruck. We both knew that our dream had gone up in smoke, but neither wanted to be the first to say so—as if putting it into words would somehow destroy all the hope of the past few months. Then we'd have to cry our hearts out.

Just then the door slammed and someone burst into the room, letting in a blast of cold air from outside. I looked up and recognized the visitor's gaunt, shrewd face under the visor of his quilted cap. "Oh, Mr. Liu!" I cried.

It was the King of the Movers. I busied myself with finding him a place to sit, while my wife put away the money that was lying on the table, as if it could talk. The King hadn't changed a bit in the six months since we'd last seen him. His bulky padded clothes made him look bloated, but his eyes, voice, and movements had the same briskness as before. He regaled us with tales of his own sagacity, which apparently contained some measure of truth, for he had just moved, and his new place rivaled that of the mighty Chief Li. And he'd also acquired a big, cheap television.

"Did Chief Li get you your new place?" I asked.

"No, he doesn't have the nerve for deals like that anymore. He got conned recently—he would've lost his job if I hadn't bailed him out."

"What? What happened?"

"Do you remember when I tried to get you to trade him a TV for an apartment six months ago, and you got cold feet? Well, if you'd done it, you'd have moved in by now, and he'd have his TV. But you doubted me.

You wouldn't listen to me—but anyway, what's done is done. You want to know what happened to Chief Li? Well, he was dying to get a TV, and he got to know some junior officer in the City Police Department. They made a deal: the cop gave him a TV, and he managed to get the cop an apartment. But before three months were up, the cop suddenly went and asked for the TV back. And he threatened to squeal on Chief Li unless he gave it back. A pretty tough cookie, wouldn't you say?"

"Wow! Really?" I exclaimed. "But if the cop squealed on Chief Li and got his TV back, wouldn't he have to give the apartment back too?"

The King accepted a cigarette from me and lit it, curling his lips in a sneer. After a couple of deep drags he said, "Don't you get it? That cop would never have squealed on Chief Li. He was just bluffing. And Chief Li knew it, but he was still scared. So he had to give in."

"Sounds like a real tough cookie!" A cold shiver ran down my spine. My wife was staring wide-eyed at the King.

"Tough? You've got to be tough! I really have to hand it to the guy. He got an apartment without forking over a single cent. What an operator! It's about time somebody taught guys like Chief Li a thing or two. Or else they'll never come down from their high horses. That's the way of the world: the tough guys with the know-how are going to come out on top, and the weaklings are going to get pushed around. Unless they just put up or shut up."

"Did Chief Li really return the TV?"

"No, he'd already given it to his son as a wedding present, so how could he take it back? Do you think his daughter-in-law would stand for a thing like that? He paid the guy back in cash."

"In cash?" cried my wife, as if she'd just discovered that she'd been gypped. Her cry brought me to my senses, and I realized that something was very wrong. My wife's tongue quavered as she asked, "Did he use his own money?"

"Who knows? He couldn't come up with four hundred bucks just then, so he tried to borrow it from me, but I didn't have it to lend. Who knows where he got it."

At this my wife and I were struck dumb. The King cast a searching glance over our blank faces. "What's up, Feng?" he asked, baffled.

I saw that there was no point in keeping the truth from him any longer, so I told him the whole story. Sheepishly, because I'd deceived him. But I just had to hear him confirm my suspicions. He didn't seem to hold it against me that I hadn't leveled with him before. He didn't even look surprised—as if people did things like that all the time. When I'd finished, he drew greedily on his cigarette until it had burned almost all the way down to his fingers. Then he stubbed it out in the ashtray. For once he didn't scoff at me, but looked concerned instead.

"Feng," he announced, "you've been had! You helped

Chief Li for nothing. He used your cash to pay off his debt, then he scraped together the money to pay you back. And you're left holding the bag."

"I'm going to go see him. He promised me!" I cried frantically.

"So what? Why didn't you snap up the apartment in the first place when you had the chance? You should've pinned him down—no apartment, no money. Now—hah! You're just wasting your time if you go see him. He doesn't owe you anything anymore, don't you see?"

"I'll report him!" I howled.

"For what? He never gave you an IOU, and he has a receipt to prove he paid you back. Besides, he returned your money in full. You didn't lose a cent, so you can't touch him. Give up, brother! You can't say you didn't have your chance. But you blew it!"

Anger, remorse, and the feeling that I'd been gypped all rolled into one. I was burned up, but there was nothing I could do. I didn't dare turn to look at my wife for fear of seeing the resentment and disappointment on her face. The King of the Movers did his best to comfort me. Filling me with new hopes and promises, he took the opportunity to point out that he was the only one I could rely on for help. Then, asking my wife to buy him five bezoar uterus pills, he stood up and left.

After we had seen him out, we sat there looking at each other, not knowing what to say. I turned the whole thing over a couple of times in my mind trying to figure out what was what. I could have kicked myself for letting such a golden opportunity slip by. Rapping my knuckles on my head, I cursed myself from the bottom of my heart: "Oh, what a numbskull I am!"

I knew that we would have to come back down from the clouds to the real world of our hassles and bickering. Events had proved my idiocy and incompetence, and now my wife would want out for sure. Things would be even worse than before.

I noticed that she was standing beside me. I glanced up at her and was amazed at what I saw. She'd never looked at me like that before—her darkly ringed eyes were sparkling with tears and tender, womanly sympathy—as if she'd discovered that I, the "Numbskull," was worthy of her love.

I'd lost one thing, but gained another.

The Hornets' Nest

Grandfather's little backyard, where hardly anyone ever went except to store odds and ends, was a gloomy jungle of untended plants and trees. But birds, butterflies, and insects frolicked there, and it was the paradise of my childhood. I liked to pluck the delicate cicada skins from the damp mossy tree trunks, to dig earthworms fat as chopsticks from the ground, and to drive clouds of flying baby grasshoppers into the spider webs. And the crab apples that weighed down the tree there were always bigger than store-bought ones.

The grandest sight of all was the hornets' nest in the eaves over Grandfather's window. Like a giant upside-down lotus seedpod, it hung there swarming with more than a hundred busy golden hornets. Grandfather was afraid to open the window because one might venture into the room.

"Damn those hornets! We can't even let any fresh air into this room. One of these days we ought to get someone to knock that nest down." Grandmother was always grumbling about the hornets' nest.

"Impossible. They'll sting the living daylights out of you," said Grandfather.

"What do you mean 'impossible'?" Grandmother retorted. "Just cover your head with a cloth, jab the nest with a pole, and that'll be that."

"Out of the question." Grandfather shook his head.

Listening to them, I got a mischievous urge to knock the nest down myself. What fun! Acting on my impulse, I went and got my little sister, and while Grandfather was taking his nap I crept into the small passageway that led to the backyard. I covered my head with my jacket, buttoning it over my nose so that only my eyes were exposed. Then I lashed two bamboo poles together for my weapon. My sister agreed to stand guard in the doorway. As soon as I had knocked down the hornets' nest, she was to let me in and shut the door behind me.

My sister kept the door open a crack to watch my deed of derring-do. Although I was having second thoughts by then, my curiosity ultimately got the better of my cowardice. Just as my poles touched the hornets' nest, I thought I heard Grandfather calling me from inside, but I was already beyond the point of no return. Some startled hornets buzzed out of the nest. I gave it two quick, hard shoves with my poles. It thudded to the ground and up swarmed a cloud of yellow hornets. Tossing my poles aside, I ran for the door, but my terrified sister had bolted it from the inside and run away. I was locked out. I turned and saw a ferocious hornet coming straight at me like a kamikaze. Petrified, I raised my hand to protect my face, but just then I felt a sharp pain between my eyebrows, as if I had been jabbed with a needle. I had been stung. I covered my face and screamed. I didn't see who opened the door and pulled me inside.

That night I ran a high fever. A date-sized lump, so big I could see it without a mirror, swelled up between my brows. The vinegar, wine, soy paste, Tiger Balm, and cold compresses that my family applied failed to reduce the swelling. The next day the doctor came and gave me a shot and some medicine, but I didn't begin to recover until a week later. I had never been sick for that long in all my life. For days afterward I avoided the small passageway to the backyard for fear hornets were still lying in wait for me at the door.

One day after I had finally recovered my nerve, I went to Grandfather's room, but he wasn't there. Out the window I saw him beckoning to me to join him in the yard. I bravely went outside. He pointed to a spot under the window. There lay the hornets' nest I had knocked down, but all the hornets were gone. Then he pointed to where I was standing: a hornet! I almost shrieked in terror and jumped away.

"What are you scared of? It's been dead for ages!" said Grandfather.

Upon closer inspection I saw that he was right. The hornet was lying on its back and black ants were crawling all over it.

"That's the one that stung you," said Grandfather. "A

hornet won't sting unless you make it angry, because one sting will cost it its life."

"Why did it want to sting me if it knew it was going to die?"

"It couldn't let you get away with destroying its home —it wanted to fight to the death!"

I was shocked to think that a little insect could have such passion and courage. I looked down at it again: its shell trembled in the breeze as if it had come back to life. I remembered how fearlessly it had charged at me that day, ready to die avenging itself on me, like a real hero. Confronted with the corpse of this tiny martyr, I felt sinful.

What about the rest of them, all the homeless hornets —would they come back and rebuild their house? I wished I could glue the empty nest back up again.

That year I often stood waiting in Grandfather's back-yard, but no hornets came.

The next spring a couple of hornets flew into the eaves above Grandfather's window. They landed on the sun-baked wooden casement and crawled about for a while on the remains of last year's nest. Then they flew away and never came back. And so another year passed un-eventfully.

One warm sunny day a year later Grandfather told me to look out the window: reddish yellow hornets were bustling around under the eaves. In their midst I spotted the dainty silver beginnings of a new nest.

Grandfather and I beamed at each other.

A Letter[1]

Dawn's first pale stirrings drove from the window the pitch-black curtain of night. Gradually the outlines of the furniture emerged from the murky shadows. It was a bitter cold morning in early spring. The stove had gone out before midnight; only the embers in its belly still smoldered. Like the wheezing of a bellows, the snores of Mrs. Yang from downstairs had kept him company throughout the night. The noise was at its loudest now, as she slumbered her soundest just before daybreak.

All night he had sat at his desk composing a reply to his brother's letter and imagining the horrors in store for himself. Haunted by one doubt after another, he had rejected each new version of the letter as soon as he had written it. First he had decided to spell everything out for his brother, but then, fearing that the letter might fall into the wrong hands, he had reworded it in code. Next he had written that he would plead innocent if Chen reported him, and asked his brother to back him up. But then he had realized that this was only clutching at straws, for there had been others present at the study group meeting who might testify against him and destroy his case.

His desk was strewn with crumpled, discarded letters.

He was trapped. He deeply regretted having made those remarks a dozen years ago. "It's out of my hands now," he wrote his brother in despair. And he added a few lines to his brother's wife:

Dear Sister-in-law,

My brother says you've been lying awake worrying about me for two nights running. We both owe you an apology. I'm thoroughly ashamed of myself. But, you know, we're not really all that bad. Our father was poor, and he died of exhaustion and illness in the old society. We were only able to go to college thanks to the Party and New China. We're certainly not enemies of the Party and the new society.

I guess we shouldn't have said those things in the first place. We gave certain unscrupulous people something to use against us. Our only excuse is that we were immature and frivolous. But please don't start worrying yet. Chen might not report me. He wouldn't be able to save himself by doing so—on the contrary, he'd be charged with covering up for me back then. Please relax. You've always treated me like your own flesh and blood. The thought that you're worrying about me just makes things worse. . . .

Tears rolled down his cheeks from behind his glasses and splattered onto the page.

His sister-in-law had shown him more love than a real sister ever would. Life was far from easy for her, but whenever she came to visit her parents she managed to bring him huge packages of Manchurian produce: beans, tree ears, dried mushrooms. And she always devoted three whole days of her time to cleaning his apartment, not leaving until she had set everything in order, washed his bedding, and mended his clothes. He felt a pang of loneliness. He had no one to turn to, no one to comfort him. The danger was as clear as could be: should disaster strike, all would be lost—his work, his job, his new girlfriend.

Just two days before, he had hopefully proposed to a spinster. And she had agreed to give him an answer that night.

At six-forty he rose, gathered the discarded letters from his desk, and burned them along with his brother's letter in the stove. In a nervous fever he slapped some paste on the letter to his brother and affixed a stamp. Then he proceeded to wash, eat breakfast, and get ready for work, but his night of worry had left him dazed with terror. Absentmindedly he carried the washbasin around the room with him, first setting it down on the table, then placing it back on the washstand. Next he drank the hot water for rinsing his mouth, thinking it was tea, and tried to lather up the soap with a dry wash-cloth. Then he unthinkingly stuffed his half-eaten piece of steamed bread into his pocket along with some things he needed and left for work. In the hall he patted his breast pocket to make sure he had not forgotten the letter.

He walked out onto the street. At the second intersection he made a beeline for the dark green cylindrical mailbox. As he approached it he looked around to see if anyone was watching. This narrow alley was well off the main street and almost deserted despite the rush hour. Playing nearby was a little boy in a green army jacket adorned with a huge Mao button. Approaching slowly, and at a distance of at least thirty yards, was an old woman with a big market basket, but she was looking the other way. There was no one else, except for a few bicyclists speeding to work. In the middle of the road some chickens were chasing back and forth, led by a crowing, strutting great white rooster with a wormlike object in its beak.

Relieved, he took the thing out of his breast pocket and thrust it toward the mailbox. But just as he was about to toss it in, he stopped short. It was a stiff little red booklet—his work ID! A close call. If he had mailed it, how would he ever have explained at the post office? Breaking into a cold sweat, he reached for the letter again, but his breast pocket was empty. He started in surprise and clutched at his side pockets. The fabric was slack. Next he searched his entire person, turning all his pockets inside out. Scraps of paper, ration tickets, and jingling coins and keys spilled to the ground. And the half-eaten piece of steamed bread that he had just pocketed rolled into the street. But the letter was gone—it had vanished into thin air.

"Oh, no!" he cried, and stood there gaping in horror. His pocket was lolling out like a dog's tongue, and the ground was strewn with glittering aluminum coins.

The old lady with the basket had walked right up to him and stopped to stare—at length, but without his even noticing.

Between seven-fifteen and seven-forty-five he ran back and forth twice from home to the mailbox. But the search was unavailing. In his building he rummaged through the stairwell and halls, disturbing his neighbor Mrs. Yang.

"What are you looking for, Comrade Wu?"

"A letter. Have you seen it?"

"A letter? Yes, of course."

"Where is it?" His heart pounded.

"Didn't I give it to you when you came home from work yesterday? Did you lose it?" she asked.

"Oh—no—not that one," he stammered, his heart sinking. "Another one!"

Dejected, he returned to his room. The letter was not there. On the table he found nothing but a used-up pad of stationery and an uncapped bottle of ink. The stove lid was open, and out of the crack curled a wisp of smoke —the remains of the wastepaper he had burned earlier that morning. In his confusion he wondered: had he absentmindedly burned the letter too? But right away he knew that he was indulging in wishful thinking. He had the distinct impression that he had picked the letter up from the desk, put it into his breast pocket on his way out the door, and patted it while he stood in the hallway. He could practically still feel it in his fingertips. There was no doubt about it. The letter was lost. Someone must have found it. But who? He thought of the little boy in the green jacket who had been playing by the street.

"Of course! There was nobody else around."

Bolting outside again, he made his way back to the spot where the boy had been playing, but he was gone. The boy probably lived in the neighborhood, he figured, so he found himself a spot under a nearby tree and began to wait. He glanced at his watch. It was already eight o'clock, time to be at the office, and Zhao Chang, the department chairman, had announced the day before that no one would be excused from work or allowed to be late today. But that problem paled in comparison to the matter at hand. Luckily, after about ten minutes a little boy with a green book bag slung over his shoulder popped out of a nearby door. He recognized the boy immediately by the enormous Mao button on his chest. Like a mugger he leaped out and grabbed the boy by the arm.

"Hey, have you seen my letter?"

The terrified boy took one look at Wu's ghastly expression and burst into tears.

"Quit blubbering! Just tell me where my letter is," he said, yanking on the boy's arm.

Just then a female voice called out from within a

walled courtyard, "What's the matter, Xiaoqing?" And out ran a short, sallow-faced woman with dripping hands, who was dressed in a blue-checked apron. The boy's mother, he assumed.

"Just what do you think you're doing?" she demanded.

When the boy saw her, he began to wail at the top of his lungs. Wu let go of him.

"I—uh—I lost a letter," he faltered. "This boy was playing here a little while ago, so I was asking him whether he'd seen it—"

"He grabbed me, and it really hurt," whined the coddled little boy.

"Well, you could've just asked him. What's the point of manhandling him?" grumbled the woman. "He's never done anything to you." She turned to her son. "Xiaoqing, have you seen his letter?"

"No. I haven't seen anything. He grabbed me—"

The boy continued to whimper, insisting that he had not seen the letter.

"Well, I'm sorry," said Wu, sheepishly hurrying away and leaving the woman to comfort the sobbing boy.

"What's so terrible about losing a letter?" she shrieked after him. "Does it mean that much to you? What a bully—picking on a little child. I've never seen the likes of it! I can tell you're in for trouble, mister!"

Her voice faded and was replaced by a ringing in his ears as it became clear to him that the letter had been picked up by a total stranger. And to make matters worse, he recalled, he had used official Historical Institute stationery to disguise his personal correspondence in the mails. He had not even put his own name and address on the envelope. Whoever had found it would certainly turn it in at the institute before long. He had delivered himself into the tiger's mouth.

CLEMENCY FOR THOSE WHO CONFESS!
SEVERITY FOR THOSE WHO RESIST!

This poster greeted Wu's eyes as he entered the Historical Institute. The lettering was taller than he was. The poster board was still damp with fresh paste, and the wet ink glistened. There it stood in awesome black and white, as if written with him in mind.

The institute was unusually quiet today. The courtyard and halls were empty; all the doors were locked. He opened his office and found it deserted. Sunlight streamed in from the four huge windows and reflected in a blinding glare off the big glass desktops. The heat had been turned off for the year, and there was a chill in the early morning air. A note on his desk caught his eye. It read:

Zhongyi:
Starting today our department is merging with the Modern History Department because of the new campaign. We're all over there. You'd better come right away!
In haste,
Zhao Chang

He made his way quickly to the Modern History Department office, which was twice the size of his. Qin Quan and Zhang Dingchen, his colleagues, were there with several people from the Modern History Department. Zhang had changed into the shabby faded blue jacket he always wore during political campaigns.[2] Everyone was writing busily. The room, which contained only five desks, was crowded with twice that number of people. Yet it was hushed as each worked in isolation. No one greeted him when he came in. Only Qin turned his long, thin, gloomy face halfway toward him and nodded wordlessly.

Personal relationships had turned sour overnight. Friends had proved fickle, and friendship had evaporated like water, leaving only arid, bald self-interest.

Qin was writing a big-character poster in his practiced block letters. The fist-sized heading read: "I WELCOME SEVERE CRITICISM." Below that was neat matchbox-sized writing. He always made one of these at the beginning of a campaign but never managed to ward off the ferocious attacks on himself.

Everyone else had eight-by-eleven sheets that looked like forms. Some were busily filling them in; others were musing with pen poised over paper; still others covered what they had written when they saw him come in. He refrained from trying to peek lest he should appear to have a guilty conscience.

The doorknob clicked and in came a tall, thin middle-aged man with square, black wire-rimmed glasses and a gilt pen clip glittering against his neat Mao suit. He had the businesslike manner typical of a functionary in a university, research institute, or office. Although he always kept somewhat aloof, he was widely respected for his decency. His name was Cui Jingchun, and he was chairman of the Modern History Department.

"You're late. What's the matter? Are you ill?" he asked, noting the strain on Wu's face.

"No, I'm fine—" Wu blurted out. But then he added, "I'm feeling a little faint. I think there might have been a gas leak in my apartment last night—anyway, I'm better now."

A poor liar, he nervously contradicted himself. Cui sensed at once that the strain was psychological rather than physical. Wu had never acted like this during a campaign before. What was the matter with him? Cui made a mental note of his suspicions. People's senses are always keener during a campaign; even the most oblivious extend their antennae.

"Starting today," Cui said impassively, "your Local History Department will merge with our department. A work team³ for the campaign has been formed in the institute; the chief is Comrade Lieman,⁴ from the political section. Your department chairman, Zhao Chang, has been transferred to the work team. For the time being I will be in charge of our big group here. Here—this is for you." He reached for some papers on the table behind him and handed them to Wu. "Give them back when you're finished," he said. Next he turned to Qin and said in a grave, official tone, "Qin, you come with me to the work team. They want to see you over there."

"All right," agreed Qin. Such a summons obviously boded ill, but he was experienced enough not to panic. Coolly he put the cap on his writing brush, folded his unfinished poster into thirds, and weighted it with his ink box. Then he picked up his teacup from the desk and gulped down some hot water as noisily as if it were a cobblestone. Replacing the cup, he followed Cui out of the room.

Wu found the atmosphere highly stressful. Taking Qin's empty seat, he looked at the papers Cui had given him. There were two mimeographed forms. One was headed:

DENUNCIATION REPORT

and at the top was printed:

Denouncer————————

Denounced————————

and:

IT IS A SERVICE TO DENOUNCE

IT IS A CRIME TO COVER UP

The other form was entitled:

STATEMENT OF CONFESSION

and it was captioned:

Confessor————————

and:

CLEMENCY FOR THOSE WHO CONFESS

SEVERITY FOR THOSE WHO RESIST

He found the blank Statement of Confession form particularly threatening.

He stared at the willow tree outside the window. Its pale green, bud-covered branches were swaying in the breeze, and yet he remained unmoved by its beauty. His mind was racing like an engine. The thought of all the disasters that the lost letter could bring sent cold shivers down his spine. Like a timid child, he let his imagination run away with him.

Suddenly it struck him that he had forgotten to check underneath his bottom desk drawer, which often spilled some of its contents out the back. In his confusion this morning he might well have shoved the letter into the drawer, in which case it would have slipped out the back if he had opened the drawer a second time. And the impression that he had put the letter into his pocket might be no more than a figment of his imagination. People often hallucinated under stress. He longed to run home and turn the desk upside down. He could hardly sit still. It even occurred to him to feign illness to get leave from work.

But getting a grip on himself again, he decided that this was mere wishful thinking. The sensation of patting the letter in his pocket as he had stood in his hallway early that morning came back to him persistently, clearly, undeniably. The letter was obviously lost. All he could do was pray that the finder would have the kindness to put it into a mailbox for him. But what if he didn't? If the finder should open it and use his secret as political capital, he would be ruined. A terrifying picture floated before his eyes: Comrade Lieman, chief of the work team, had gotten the letter from an informer and was now opening it. . . .

There was a knock at the door. He panicked.

"Come in," called one of his colleagues.

The door opened a crack and in peered a man with the ponderous face, droopy little eyes, and big thick lips of a hippo.

"Is this the office?" he asked with a Sichuan accent. "I'm here on business."

"We're having a campaign here. You'd better take your business to the revolutionary committee on the second floor of the rear building. If you're checking someone's references, go to the third floor. That's where the work team is," the colleague said flatly. At a time like this nobody wanted to go poking his nose into other people's business.

Wu was sitting directly across from the door. He caught a glimpse of something white in the man's hand. His heart leaped into his throat. Had the man come to turn in his letter?

The man had shut the door and was gone.

Wu scrambled noisily to his feet, almost overturning his chair in the process, and dashed out into the hall, leaving his colleagues baffled. At the door at the end of the hall he caught up with the man.

"Who do you want to talk to?"

"The heads of your institute."

"Uh—is that a letter you have there?"

"Yes."

"Did you by any chance find it in the street?"

"Find it?" The man squinted in amazement. "What are you talking about? I'm here on business from the Chongqing Museum. This is my letter of introduction. If you don't believe me, just look—here's the official stamp. And I have my work ID with me." Frowning, he unfolded the white piece of paper in his hand. It was indeed a letter of introduction. And it bore the round vermilion stamp of the museum.

Wu breathed a sigh of relief, but then he noticed the man's extreme discomfiture. His mouth twitching with embarrassment, he made the necessary apologies. A clear explanation, however, was out of the question.

"Of all the nerve," muttered the man, huffily striding away.

As Wu turned back he saw Zhao approaching him.

"Say, I hear you're filling out a denunciation report," Zhao said, smiling. "You'd better let me see it when you're finished."

"What? Denunciation? A denunciation of what?" he asked, bewildered.

"Why, a denunciation of me, of course. What are you gawking at? I'm just kidding. Besides, you wouldn't give me your denunciation report anyway. You have to give it to Cui, but I'll see it eventually—hey, don't take me seriously! You and I know perfectly well that we're both clean, don't we?" He patted Wu affectionately. "If you need anything, I'm in the work team office on the third floor of the rear building. Oh, and how come you were late this morning? I didn't see you, so I left a note on your desk. I guess you must have gotten it." And he walked away without waiting for Wu's reply.

Wu was indescribably relieved. Wasn't Zhao's affection a sign that the work team hadn't seen his letter? He might as well look on the bright side as long as he could. If only he could forget about the letter and bask forever in Zhao's affection, as in a hot shower, never facing reality soberly again. He and Zhao were the best of friends. Zhao had often patted his skinny shoulder with his soft pudgy hand, but never had the gesture meant as much to him as it had today.

But what had Zhao meant by those remarks?

He would probably never find out as long as he lived.

Two hearts may fuse on contact, like raindrops, but they may also be as far apart as stars. From the vantage point of one, the other may be shrouded in mystery, an insoluble riddle. . . .

Strange to say, Zhao was actually afraid of Wu until he discovered Wu's secret.

Zhao, a fat, flabby, fiftyish man, had started out in the Business Office of the Utilities Bureau, but his true interest was local history. He spent his spare time interviewing old people and collecting curios, fragmentary materials, out-of-print books, the letters of local dignitaries, posters from peasant movements, New Year's folk paintings, bricks and tiles, old photographs, and so on.

Gradually he had gained recognition as an amateur

specialist. After the institute established a Department of Local History in 1958, he was transferred there along with Zhang. Qin, who was one of the original employees of the institute, had been charged with rightism in 1957 and assigned to the department after his name was cleared. The last to join was Wu Zhongyi.

Human relations work like lock and key: a lock will spring open as long as the key fits. Zhao was amiable and hardworking. He was Wu's kind of man, and he and Wu made friends quickly.

Before Wu's arrival, the three-member Local History Department, headed informally by Zhao, had been affiliated with the Modern History Department under Cui. When the separate Local History Department was established after Wu's arrival, Wu was appointed temporary chairman on the strength of his college degree and Youth League membership. Zhao, Zhang, and Qin had no such political credentials. The post was designated "temporary" because of his brother's bad record, but there was no one to replace him.

Zhao showed no sign of jealousy toward the outsider who had been appointed chairman. On the contrary, he admired Wu's scholarship. Since he himself had started out as an amateur, he regarded Wu as his mentor.

Wu's ability, however, was evident only in his professional research. In his personal life he was absentminded. Although he could reel off the names of all the dynasties and imperial reigns backward, practical matters invariably slipped his mind, and his daily life was haphazard. He constantly misplaced his umbrellas, pens, handkerchiefs, scarves, and face masks; and since he frequently lost his keys, his door bore the scars of many forcible entries.

Although he was single and did not want for money, he lived poorly and dressed shabbily. People always assumed he was just making a show of poverty, but in fact he hardly ever ate a decent meal. Zhao, who was more worldly, helped him out. Every winter Zhao would install the chimney of Wu's stove. And since Wu was particularly inept at dealing with people, Zhao regularly helped to extricate him whenever he got into a bind. Gradually he came to rely on Zhao.

Once as he gazed gratefully at Zhao's pudgy face, Zhao mocked him, "You won't need your friends anymore once you find a wife."

Wu shook his head. For many years he had been too cautious to make any friends. But a long acquaintanceship with Zhao had convinced him that Zhao was honest and reliable, and he had come to regard him as a friend and to believe that their friendship would last forever.

Then came the Cultural Revolution, sweeping away everything, tangibles and intangibles, in its path. In the beginning, when people were to rebel against the leadership, Zhao attacked Wu with a big-character poster that read: "The department chairman values work over politics, practices apolitical professionalism . . ." etc., and mentioned a few examples. Wu was shocked. He could not understand why Zhao would do such a thing. Zhao's poster was the opening volley, and Zhang and two members of the Ming History Department soon followed suit.

Wu lay awake at night in fear. But thanks to his usual circumspection, they were unable to find much ammunition, and the trouble ended as quickly as it had begun. He soon forgot about it. He was not the type to hold a grudge. Still, Zhao's behavior had definitely caused a rift. Slowly they drifted apart.

Then the armed factional fighting broke out, and Zhao became a hard-core activist in Lieman's faction. The opposing side, believing him to be an organizer, seized him, bundled him up in a burlap sack, and beat him mercilessly. To Wu, a neutral observer, Zhao's fanaticism was baffling. On one occasion Zhao tried to persuade him to join his faction, but he politely refused. He had never before rejected one of Zhao's suggestions. They drifted even further apart. For a long time Zhao did not drop by to visit.

Then came the truce and work returned to normal. To Zhao's faction, the victors, went the lion's share of the new leadership appointments. Lieman was named chief of the political section, and Zhao became chairman of the Local History Department. Wu, the original chairman, while not formally dismissed, was simply swept aside in the shuffle. Although Wu heard the rumor that Zhao had always coveted his job, he did not believe it. All that mattered to him now was that he was safe. Terrorized by two years of internecine strife, he longed to bury his head in the sand. He bore Zhao no ill will, just as Zhao had not begrudged him his post of temporary chairman.

On the night that Zhao was appointed department chairman he turned up at Wu's door. He looked as relaxed as ever, despite his long absence. With a friendly grin on his face he sauntered in and patted Wu affectionately on the shoulder.

"You and I haven't had a drink together in more than two years," he said with a chuckle. "It's all my fault for running around like a chicken without a head. From now on I'll be sure to drop in all the time."

With these words, a murky, unpleasant chapter in their lives was closed as if nothing had ever come between them. Zhao had brought some liquor and pickles. They set the table, sat down across from each other, and clinked their glasses together as if their old intimacy were restored. But Wu felt slightly awkward, as if he were to blame for their period of estrangement.

Wu was not much of a drinker: half a glass was enough to make him tipsy. Before long he had the feeling that he was moving someone else's foot, though in fact it was his own. He was seeing double, and under the lamplight Zhao's face looked like a big, downy, white ball with human features. Wu smiled but remained silent, for alcohol tended to seal his lips.

Although Zhao was a better drinker than Wu, he had also had a drop too much. His ears were ringing, his face was flushed, his head ached. He had the feeling that his companion's head was swaying, but he could not tell if it was Wu that was moving or himself. His tongue, unlike Wu's, was loosened by alcohol.

Liquor tends to knock out the guards at the doors of

the heart and release the truth. Zhao's mind was seething; his usual restraint was gone. He had the urge to cry, to yell, to unburden himself. He spat a chicken neck bone onto the table.

"You must be angry at me for putting up that big-character poster about you and taking your place as department chairman."

"Not at all!" In a drunken haze, Wu shook his head.

"Oh, come on, why don't you speak up like a true friend? I didn't want to be chairman. The job is lowly and tiring, and you always end up rubbing somebody the wrong way. It's a waste of time. They made me take it. The truth of the matter is, they didn't want you because your brother was a rightist. Actually you should be glad you're not chairman. From now on, people like you who have political offenders in the family had better lie low. Just do your work and go home. And as for that big-character poster I put up about you, I—" Zhao flung his glass down on the table. His fat red face was impassioned; his small eyes shimmered with tears.

"I admit it was selfish of me," he continued, his lips quivering. "I'm sorry. Here's what happened. I heard a rumor that you had a political offender in your family, and you had always been more concerned with your work than with politics. Director Hao—well, I might as well tell you—he was afraid he was going to be ousted, so he decided to use you as a red herring. When I heard he was gathering information to mount a campaign against you, I was afraid I'd be dragged into it, since everybody knew we were friends. So I put up that poster. So there it is. Now it's up to you. If you want to hate me for it, go ahead. You have every right to hate me, and I deserve it."

Wu was tingling all over with alcohol. He was appalled, yet he could not bear to listen to anyone beg his forgiveness. Moved to tears, as though Zhao had granted him a special favor, he lifted his glass.

"Let's let bygones be bygones," he said with unaccustomed warmth. "I—I propose a toast."

Zhao snatched up his glass and filled it, and they drained the toast, plunging themselves deeper still into an alcoholic stupor.

"You're so forgiving, I don't know what to say," sobbed Zhao. "Trust me. From now on I promise I'll do right by you. Please don't think I'm the kind of person who gets ahead by stepping all over other people. And I'll tell you something else—I've seen through everything that's happened in the last two years. In the beginning I thought the campaign was exciting: revolution, life-and-death struggle, everybody on the warpath. It seems ridiculous to me now that I, a full-grown man, would get involved in childish gang fights and stay out at all hours like a man possessed, turning a deaf ear to everybody. I was too refined to get into fights when I was young, but I sure got my head smashed in after I grew up.

"Now the two factions have arrived at a truce. But when you stop to think, what were we fighting about? Today I'm the enemy, tomorrow it's your turn. And it's all for nothing. What's the point? We're just a bunch of pawns. They arrange us on the chessboard and we fight. When they don't need us anymore they put us away. The more I think about it, the more pointless it seems."

To Wu, Zhao's face was a blur, and he could hardly hear what was being said. But instinct warned him that Zhao was skating on thin ice. He shook his head vigorously.

"You'd better watch out. Think before you speak. Or you'll be ruined for life." His speech was thick, and his tongue stumbled over the words.

A tiny spot in Zhao's sodden brain still clung to sobriety. He shuddered, as with an electric shock, and the fog in his mind lifted momentarily. He fixed his wide bloodshot eyes on Wu.

Wu was still shaking his head. Even his shoulders were swaying, as though he were aboard a tossing ship.

"It's terrible," he was mumbling. "What you just said is react—react—"

"Reactionary? Why, what did I say?"

Wu suddenly lost his balance and lurched to the left, steadying himself against the back of his chair. Without the armrest, he would have fallen to the floor. Dead-drunk, he was unable to answer, no matter how Zhao pleaded with him.

Zhao helped him to bed and departed gloomily. His indiscretion weighed on his mind all the way home. He despised alcohol, but above all he was disgusted with himself.

Wu never mentioned the incident again.

Neither did Zhao. If Wu had been too drunk that

night to understand what he had said, then he had best not spell it out for him. Besides, there would ordinarily have been nothing dreadful about making such remarks, especially to someone like Wu, who liked to stay out of trouble. And Wu was a good friend, who would never dream of reporting him. But things were different during a campaign. Those few remarks were enough to seal his fate. He had to be on guard against anyone who knew his weak spots. So he decided to keep an eye on Wu. He set up a secret, invisible cordon.

But Wu was totally unsuspecting. His own problems were more than he could handle. Besides, he had been in such a drunken fog that night that Zhao's remarks had slipped his mind altogether.

That evening Wu stood by the river. A gentle breeze caressed his face; the cool night air was laden with the refreshing smells of early spring. Silvery moonbeams flashed on the rippling water, outlining him, the railing, and the bushes in picturesque silhouette. Lofty poplar trees rustled all around, masking the whispers of the couples hidden in the shadows. Under the moonlight a thin, frail woman was slowly and shyly making her way toward him. Like the sweet strains of a zither, the enchanting moonlit evening accompanied her graceful approach.

But all this seemed to have nothing to do with him.

After work he had hurried home and removed all his desk drawers to expose the dark space at the bottom. But he had found only an old photo, a little plastic notebook cover, some staples, and a couple of pages from a useless manuscript. The letter was not there. In despair and confusion he had come to the banks of the river to keep his date with his girlfriend.

Only a few days before, he had been making blissful plans to marry this woman and set up housekeeping. A couple of years ago he had been a confirmed bachelor, but meeting her at the end of last year had changed his mind. Although she was simple and weak, unlike his sister-in-law, she was honest and reliable—just the kind of woman he happened to like. Maybe he was afraid that a smarter woman would boss him around. He pictured his future: he would do his research at a desk with a lamp, surrounded by books in a warm, cozy room. And she, with a wifely smile, would set a cup of fresh hot tea before him. For him marriage was as simple as that. He wanted an understanding woman, one who would willingly shoulder the burdens of life and free him to devote himself to his beloved work. Also he hoped to enjoy a loving marriage and to have a child that would lend cheer to his hushed, lonely apartment. Besides, his marriage would be a relief to his brother and sister-in-law, who were so far away. But unless he could find the letter, his dreams would have to go up in smoke.

The woman, whose name was Li, was gazing at him. Although her large eyes were no longer youthful, they shimmered with the light of first love. She lowered her eyelids. Her heart was pounding. His, however, was numb.

Both remained silent, but for entirely different reasons.

Li was too bashful to look at him again. If she had, his wooden expression would have put her on the alert.

They walked a ways and stopped by the railing, their thoughts worlds apart. Li took something out of her pocket and silently handed it to him.

"What is it?" he asked.

"A letter," she murmured.

"A letter?" He winced at the word "letter," and his mind began to reel. How had she gotten the lost letter? "Whose?" he demanded. "Mine? Here, let me have it!"

On their last date Wu had made her a proposal of marriage, and she had agreed to consider it. This was her letter of acceptance, the first time she had ever opened her heart to a man. Mistaking Wu's eagerness for passion, she was overjoyed. Coyly she placed the letter in his hand, averted her face, and gazed at the dazzling moonlight on the river.

"This is my reply," she said softly.

"What? You mean—it's not—oh, it's from you!" The bubble had burst. His voice betrayed his disappointment.

"What's the matter?"

"Oh, nothing. That's fine," he said, tucking the letter into his pocket like a handkerchief.

She was stung to the quick. Her happy glow faded, and her skin sagged in slack folds. In the shadows of the night she looked like the old maid that she was.

She turned and walked away, and he followed dazedly.

Too absorbed in his own gloom to notice the change that had come over her, he walked in silence, as though

she were a total stranger. He followed her to an intersection.

"Give it back!" he heard her say suddenly.

"What?"

"The letter. The one I just gave you."

He took it out of his pocket. Before he knew what she
was doing, she had snatched it.

"I'm going home," she announced.

"I'll walk you there."

"Don't bother," she said in a cold, determined tone, as
if to warn him never to come near her again.

Finally coming to his senses, Wu hastily tried to mol-
lify her.

"I don't feel very well today," he explained. "Please
forgive me. Can I have the letter back?"

A streetlight illumined the hideous grin on her face.

"Don't bother," she repeated glacially. "I can see that
you've changed your mind. You don't really want it."
And she tucked the letter into her pocket and turned
away.

He stood helplessly rooted to the spot and watched
her go. Finally he forced himself to call out, "I'll come
see you tomorrow or the day after."

Turning a deaf ear to him, she quickened her stride
and rapidly disappeared from sight.

He made his way home with a heavy heart. Letters,
letters, letters! he thought. Letters of introduction, love
letters, letters everywhere. Millions of letters exchanged
hands every day, but the one letter he wanted was gone.
He had a hazy sense that disaster had already appeared

on the horizon. All he could do now was sit back and wait.

On the first day of the campaign at the institute, a mere dozen denunciations were collected, only one of which was usable: a report on an old office worker named Chen for having held his *Quotations from Chairman Mao* upside down during two Morning Salute[5] ceremonies. As a result the work team decreed that everyone had to hand in at least one denunciation report before going home each day.

By now the office had emptied out a little. One woman had been transferred from the Modern History Department to the personnel section of the work team. Qin had disappeared. Rumor had it that a detention block had been set up and that Qin and a few others who had bad records were being detained around the clock to write self-criticisms. Qin's "I WELCOME SEVERE CRITICISM" poster still lay folded in thirds under the ink box on his desk, as if he were dead.

Wu was in his seat waiting for the work team to summon him with the news that his letter had been turned in. He had visions of confessing, enduring a public criticism session, and joining Qin in the detention block.

He stared at the denunciation report before him. He had to fill it in, but his mind was blank. He was on pins and needles. Restlessly he shifted his weight in his chair. Everyone else was fidgeting too.

Time ticked by, empty and tedious.

Cui came in. Everyone stared at his own denunciation report, pretending to be lost in thought. Then Zhang stood up and deferentially handed two sheets of paper to Cui.

"This is a petition," he stammered. "I would like the leadership to deduct ten dollars from my salary every month so that I can pay back the interest I received for ten years.[6] It was obtained through exploitation and was not rightly mine in the first place, so I want to return it. And this is a denunciation of my uncle, who had a rice shop before liberation and cut the rice with sand to cheat the laboring masses. All the details are here."

Cui listened impassively.

"Where's your uncle now?" he asked.

"He died. In 1959."

"What are you denouncing him for if he's dead?" Scorn flickered across Cui's deadpan face. He took the papers and left.

Zhang returned to his seat and sat wide-eyed, mulling over Cui's response.

Wu was still trying to fill in his denunciation report, yet he could not stop worrying about the letter long enough to think of anything to write. Without realizing what he was doing, he doodled the word "letter" on his report. He panicked: such an unlucky slip could betray him. Quickly he blotted it out with ink.

Just then Zhao came in. Wu hurriedly folded up his denunciation report and covered it with his hand as if it were a live locust. Zhao plumped down on the chair next to him.

"What have you written? Can I see?" He chuckled.

Hastily protesting that he had written nothing, Wu clutched his report and refused to let Zhao see it. Tension and fear showed on his face.

Zhao warily assumed that he had caught Wu red-handed in the act of reporting his drunken indiscretion. But he merely patted Wu on the shoulder and smiled as if nothing were wrong.

"Just remember," he said, "honesty is the best policy. You're just asking for it if you make wild accusations. Well, I'll let you get on with your writing. See you later." He rose and left.

He paused for a moment in the hall. Fishing out a cigarette, he took a few puffs and began to exhale wreaths of smoke, smoke that whirled like the fog of suspicions in his mind. He racked his brains for an explanation of Wu's peculiar behavior. In all likelihood, he figured, his worst fears were justified: Wu was going to report his indiscretion and have him stripped of his title of department chairman. Leaving a drifting cloud of smoke in the hallway, he hurried back to his room to plan his counterattack.

Wu and Zhao spent the next two days in mutual doubt and fear.

Zhao gave Wu the cold shoulder whenever they met. Without so much as a glance at Wu, he would nod almost imperceptibly and brush past him. He wanted to put pressure on Wu, to let Wu know that he was aware of his intentions. And at the close of every day he waited in the work team office for Cui to bring the denunciations from the Modern History Department so that he could see whether Wu had reported him.

Zhao's behavior worried Wu, who thought that the lost letter must have been turned in to the work team and that Zhao had discovered his secret. He figured that because they were such close friends, Zhao would try to protect himself by putting distance between them, just as he had done before when he had put up that big-character poster.

Wu interpreted his friend's manner as a barometer of his own situation—which proved disastrous, since Zhao was doing exactly the same thing.

Wu was tense, especially when he saw Zhao. Behind his glasses his nervous little gray eyes rolled like marbles, furtively avoiding Zhao's gaze.

So, you little punk, thought Zhao, you're scared of me, and you've already made your opening move.

It occurred to Zhao that Cui might have deliberately hidden Wu's denunciation report from him and might even have passed it on behind his back to Lieman, the chief of the work team. He began to keep an eye on both Lieman and Cui. He hated Wu's guts. If only Wu would suddenly be taken ill, he thought, or have an accident on the way to or from work, or make a mistake so that he could nab him and finish him off before he could turn around and bite back.

———

Comrade Lieman was a tyrant. He was a paltry political-section chief, a twenty-first-grade personnel cadre, who rode a cheap rusty bicycle to work every day, could not afford the good food in the cafeteria, and had to run around asking people to buy medicine for him when he was sick—just like everyone else. But in those extraordinary times, when the personnel section[7] reigned supreme, he wielded tremendous power.

Persecution had become his main purpose in life. He had absolute control over people's relationships. Any contact with him spelled disaster. Although this meant he was an outcast, he was quite content to liken himself to "concentrated pesticide." The pesticide, however, had been sprayed indiscriminately, sending even harmless insects running for cover.

He was shrewd. He knew how to read people's minds, how to extract their secrets. He was as clever as a cricket catcher who coaxes his prey out of chinks in a wall.

People like him were bred by an abnormal society, and they in turn contributed to its malaise. In those years when solid work was not valued, his kind proliferated until they virtually constituted a profession. Such people created a stifling, fear-ridden atmosphere.

They were afflicted with an occupational disease: In ordinary times they were lonely and bored, but a campaign stimulated them like a drug. They were like creatures of the night, who begin to stir after dusk. Lieman was exhilarated now, as energized as an athlete just come out on the field.

One morning Zhang wrote a self-critical big-character poster which read: "SEVERELY CRITICIZE MY EXPLOITATIVE CRIME." Wu offered to help him post it in the courtyard.

He went because he was too nervous to sit in the office and wanted to see if there was anything about himself among the posters in the yard. Also he hoped against hope that somehow he might intercept the finder of his letter there.

Posters covered the walls of the yard: pledges, promises, critiques, attacks, rebuttals, defections, and exposés. All dealt with picayune factional squabbles, in terms ranging from innuendos to specifics. Here conflicts were aired, intensified, and deepened, or rather, they were intensified and deepened by being aired.

Wu and Zhang found a space, applied paste, and put up Zhang's poster. Then Zhang decided that it was crooked and reached up with his delicate white hands to straighten it. Wu, paste jar in hand, stood to one side to tell Zhang when it looked right.

Suddenly Wu had the sensation that someone was standing beside him. He turned and found Lieman, hands clasped behind his back, drilling into him with his eyes. Wu panicked, and the paste jar fell to the ground with a thud.

Lieman smiled inscrutably; he looked faintly sardonic.

For several seconds Wu stood paralyzed with fear before squatting down to clean up the sticky, slippery mess with trembling hands. He managed to glance up at Lieman with a forced smile.

"The handle was slippery, and I—" he said.

Lieman turned away without a word. There was no need to ask questions. He had already been handed a tremendous windfall.

Back at the work team office, Zhao was sorting denunciation reports. Lieman sat down, lit a cigarette, and smoked for a while.

"Say, what do you think of Wu?" he asked, with his back to Zhao.

Zhao winced, sensing that Lieman might have had some contact with Wu. Could Lieman have found out about his own indiscretion? he wondered. Was this a test? His limbs went dead. Terror flitted across his face, but luck was with him: this momentary lapse escaped Lieman's notice. Quickly he lowered his eyes and began to leaf through the papers on his desk.

"Uh—I don't know."

"What do you mean? Aren't you his friend?" Lieman asked, spinning around to face him.

"Friend?" Zhao snorted. "He's like that with everybody."

"I thought you looked out for him."

"Well, we're in the same department, and we have research interests in common, so naturally we're close—"

"But aren't you the one who sets up his stove every winter? And you lent him twenty dollars a couple of months ago when his brother was sick, didn't you?" Lieman's gaze bored into him.

Zhao was taken aback, but then he reminded himself that Lieman had always made it his business to keep track of who was friendly with whom in the institute and of how people spent their spare time. He had been in Lieman's faction early in the Cultural Revolution, and Lieman had valued him then—he had transferred him to the work team. But he was well aware that this was only because Lieman had not caught him making any mistakes. Lieman would not spare his closest friends or relatives if they happened to slip up. Why had Lieman raised this subject? he wondered. No good could come of it.

"Yes, he asked me to lend it to him." He was hedging. "I couldn't very well refuse. That was just common courtesy."

"Do you know his private thoughts?"

It began to dawn on Zhao that Lieman's questions had nothing to do with himself. Relieved, he started to speak more smoothly.

"Well, even though it might look as though we're pretty good friends, I don't really know what makes him tick. He and I usually just talk shop. He never lets me in on his personal affairs or private opinions. Sometimes he sighs, but he won't tell me what's wrong. By now I've stopped even asking," he answered in an attempt to deflect Lieman's suspicions.

Lieman changed his tack. "Can he get shortwave broadcasts on his radio?"

"I don't think so. I don't think he even has a radio," answered Zhao. Although he could not tell what Lieman was driving at, he was now certain that the grilling was not aimed at him.

"Does he keep a diary?" asked Lieman.

"I don't know. If he did, he wouldn't let me see it. What's up? Why do you ask?" Zhao inquired, trying to seize the initiative.

Lieman sprang to his feet.

"He's done something wrong!" he announced.

Zhao's eyes shone with relief. Still, he wondered, how could Lieman find fault with a timid soul like Wu, who always played by the rules?

"What on earth has he done?" he asked.

Lieman glanced at him without answering. Cigarette in hand, he began to pace back and forth. Then he stopped at the desk, crushed out his cigarette in a glass ashtray, and turned to face Zhao.

"Never mind about that for now," he said. "I'm sure he's done something. I need someone to keep tabs on him to see if there's anything fishy about his behavior and to keep me informed if there is. I'm giving you the assignment because you're on pretty good terms with him. He won't get suspicious if you hang around him. But he is not to be alarmed, no matter what. Do you think you can handle it?"

Zhao was delighted. Wu had not reported him after all. And this assignment would give him the upper hand on Wu.

"Yes, I can," he answered. "But would you please let Cui in on this? Or else he'll get suspicious of me for hanging around Wu. And Cui is such a strange fellow."

" 'Strange' is hardly the word for him. He's a right-wing conservative, an opponent of class struggle. But that's beside the point. Starting tomorrow you'll join the Modern History Department in your capacity as a work team member. Okay?"

"Okay! Fine!" Zhao was poised for the attack.

Zhao sat in the Modern History Department office spying on Wu.

Wu did indeed seem distraught: his face was as white as a sheet, and his eyes, behind his glasses, studiously avoided Zhao's gaze. He would stare vacantly out the window or into a corner for half an hour at a time, while a terrified, anguished look kept passing across his face. If anyone called his name or made a sudden noise, he would quiver like a startled sparrow.

These, Zhao realized, were the symptoms of preoccupation. Wu was ordinarily slovenly; that was nothing new. But now, Zhao noticed, his face was dirty, his eyes gummy with sleep, his neck grimy. He had not washed thoroughly in four or five days. Nor had a comb come near his hair, which was matted like a heap of straw. He had dark circles under his eyes and had lost so much weight that his cheekbones stuck out like a reef at low tide.

Does he have insomnia? wondered Zhao. What on earth is the matter? Could his conscience really be bothering him?

Zhao began to pity his old friend. A dozen years' friendship had taught him that Wu did not have a mean bone in his body. He simply could not bring himself to hate Wu. In fact, he had an urge to have a private, no-holds-barred talk with him, to try to help him. But that was out of the question. If Wu was in serious trouble, he himself might be implicated. Besides, he couldn't exclude the possibility that Wu might report him. The bigger Wu's problems were, the more likely he was to talk to save his own skin.

Before lunch Cui asked Wu to leave the room with him for a chat. Zhao followed them. After prowling around in the corridor, he found them talking in the empty Local History Department office. He paused outside the door to eavesdrop, but they were beyond earshot.

At lunch in the steamy, bustling cafeteria, Zhao spotted Cui eating alone at a table. He carried his lunch box over, sat down beside him, and began to eat.

"What did you want with Wu just now?" he whispered.

"Nothing," Cui answered dryly, glancing up at Zhao. "We just had a little chat."

"What did he say?"

"Nothing," Cui repeated, glancing at Zhao again.

Was it about me? Zhao wondered. His suspicion of Wu flared up again, replacing the pity he had felt earlier. He would have to polish Wu off quickly now if he wanted to preserve himself.

He gobbled down his lunch and went back to the work team to report an exaggerated version of his findings to Lieman.

"I'll tell Cui to put the screws to him," Lieman said, nodding and cackling with glee.

"I'm not sure Cui is up to it," observed Zhao, launching into an account of Cui's tête-à-tête with Wu in the Local History Department office before lunch. "I think you were right yesterday when you said that Cui's heart isn't in the campaign," he added. "In my opinion they're far too lax over there at the Modern History Department. And Cui didn't seem too happy to have me there."

Lieman's face stiffened with rage.

"Well then," he crowed, "I'll put the screws to him myself. I've arranged a very interesting assembly for tomorrow, and it's been approved by the leadership. You'll see! I guarantee you that the fish are going to come leaping out of the water all on their own."

The next day the courtyard of the Historical Institute was as grim as an execution ground.

All the employees were seated in rows on the ground. The cement platform at the main entrance to the rear building had been converted into a temporary rostrum. There were no decorations; beauty was as superfluous here as in a fort—where nothing matters but firepower.

In the center of the rostrum was a wooden table without a tablecloth, on which stood a drumstick-shaped microphone wrapped in red fabric. In a line of wooden chairs at the door sat the stony-faced leaders of the institute.

Lieman, in a green army cap, swaggered onto the rostrum and stood at attention behind the table for three minutes. A hush fell over the crowd. Suddenly he pounded on the table. Everyone flinched.

"Bring in the reactionary right-wingers, the former counterrevolutionaries: Qin and his three cohorts!" he barked out.

An answering cry rang out from the corner of the building, and in marched paired institute militiamen with red "On Duty" armbands on their army jackets, holding Qin and the others by twisting their arms up behind their backs. Meanwhile, a man and a woman at the corner of the rostrum led the audience in chanting slogans, and a sea of little white fists rose and fell in cadence. At once the atmosphere was raised to a fever pitch.

Wu sat in the crowd imagining that he too might be forced up onstage within the next few days. He broke into a cold sweat.

Zhao, who was sitting on Wu's left, was observing his reactions out of the corner of his right eye.

Qin and the others took their places onstage with heads bowed, and the criticism session began. Some hardcore activists who had stayed up all night preparing speeches to order took turns onstage denouncing the counterrevolutionaries. Next, to the roar of shouted slogans, the paired militiamen escorted Qin and the others offstage, and Lieman returned.

"Now we've publicly denounced Qin and the other three scoundrels," he began, propping his arms on the table. "However, the target of this campaign is not these four but the enemy hidden deep within. The campaign began almost a week ago. At that time we distributed two forms: a denunciation and a confession. I am going to announce the results, because our work is open and aboveboard. We have no secrets. By now we've gotten lots of denunciations but hardly any confessions. We've conducted a very productive preliminary investigation of the leads in the denunciations we have received, including some from other organizations. We have ample evidence that there are a number of counter-revolutionaries, both old and new, lurking in our institute. They are in your midst right now!"

Lieman spoke extemporaneously; the words rolled easily off his tongue and produced the desired result. The audience was absolutely still. Wu felt as though every word were directed at him. He heard the rest of Lieman's speech only above a ringing in his ears.

"For the past few days we have enjoined these people repeatedly to come forward and confess, to choose leniency for themselves. But things have not turned out as we had hoped. Some of these people are taking a gamble. They think that we're bluffing or that they can give us the slip. Others refuse to come clean and seem determined to brazen it out. We have no choice but to take action. Time is of the essence. We can't just sit back and let these people go on getting away with murder. Today we're going to nab a few of them right here to show you we mean business!"

Wu sat transfixed, as though carved in wood, his gaze riveted on Lieman. Only his eyelids were still moving.

As he sat by Wu's side, Zhao was having qualms of his own. Lieman still seemed to trust him, he thought. He had been unable to detect any change in Lieman's attitude toward him. Still, no one was safe at a time like this. Disaster could take you completely unawares. How did he know that Lieman was showing his true colors? A man like Lieman was unfathomable. . . . Bathed in the spring sun, Zhao's forehead oozed sweat. Whether the sweat was cold or warm he did not know.

"To give these people a last chance to confess," Lieman was haranguing the crowd, "I'm going to stand here and wait for five minutes. If you haven't turned yourselves in when the time is up, we'll have to seize you. Our policy distinguishes very clearly: those who confess voluntarily will be shown clemency, but those whom we have to single out will be punished severely. All right—" Lifting his wrist to look at his watch, he called out like a sports referee:

"Begin!"

The hushed audience waited in terror, as during the five minutes before an execution.

"Four more minutes," announced Lieman. "Three minutes—two minutes—a minute and a half—thirty seconds—five seconds—"

Wu had closed his eyes as though waiting for a bullet to be fired at his breast.

"Bang!" Lieman struck the table and bellowed, "Arrest the former counterrevolutionary Wang Qianlong!"

A pair of militiamen with red armbands, who had been standing ready, charged into the left side of the crowd, seized a short, thin, gray-haired man, and forced him onto the stage, while the slogan leaders led the entire audience in chanting the slogans on their handouts. Wu glanced up at Wang Qianlong. He could not help starting in surprise: he had never dreamed that this prudent, sickly old scholar from the Ming History Department was a former counterrevolutionary.

Head bowed, Wang took his position onstage. Then Lieman, his eyes glinting under the visor of his army cap, began to survey the crowd. His gaze stopped at Wu, whereupon he reached out one hand and pointed directly at him. With his other hand he pounded on the table again. Wu's heart missed a beat.

"Arrest the evil chief of the reactionary clique, the active counterrevolutionary Wang Jihong!" roared Lieman. Wang Jihong was sitting directly behind Wu.

Two militiamen trotted over, grabbed Wang Jihong as if he were a little bird, and forced him up onstage next to Wang Qianlong. Like a searchlight, Lieman's gaze slowly continued to scan the faces in the audience. Then he banged on the table and shouted once more, and someone else was brought onstage to the accompaniment of slogan chanting.

Just as he was about to strike the table again, a round-headed, bespectacled man stood up in the audience. It was Zhang.

"I have something to confess," he said in a quavering, breathless voice. "I handed over my savings when my house was searched in 1966, but I hid a pair of gold bracelets and a jade ring in the coal heap. And I said to my wife in private that the revolutionary masses who had searched my house were bandits."

"All right," said Lieman after a brief silence. "We welcome your voluntary confession. Come forward please. Stand over here. Did everybody see that? Our policy distinguishes clearly: different treatment for different behavior. But I know there are more criminals and counterrevolutionaries among you. If you don't turn yourselves in we'll have to seize you!" And he continued his slow scan of the crowd.

Despite his terror, Wu simply could not bring himself to stand up and confess.

Zhao had never seen such cruelty. Before his very eyes members of the audience were being called by name, seized, and lined up onstage. They were ruined. Maybe Lieman would call his name next. Suddenly it occurred to him to turn to Wu and ask him quietly whether he had informed on him. If Wu had, he might as well stand up and confess. But he controlled himself, and gradually his reason and experience got the better of his momentary panic. He decided to stick to his guns: better to be seized and dealt with harshly than to let Lieman call his bluff.

The sweat on his forehead collected into one big drop, which trickled down his cheek. He had forgotten his handkerchief, however, so he reached over to borrow one from Wu. But before he could tell Wu what he wanted, Lieman's hand had banged down on the table again. Zhao flinched.

Wu flinched too and unconsciously clutched Zhao's outstretched hand. When Zhao felt Wu's clammy, trembling touch, he decided for certain that Wu must be concealing a terrible secret.

This time Lieman seized a young man from the reference room who had been reported for a slip of the tongue. Zhao knew about the case because he had seen the informant's report among the denunciations.

Wu relaxed slightly when he saw that it was not his turn.

But his panicky behavior had placed him next in line. After the assembly Zhao reported Wu's reactions to Lieman, who resolved to use the momentum created by the assembly to get to the bottom of Wu's secret.

Fifteen minutes later, Zhao and Lieman barged into the Modern History Department as though they had a warrant for someone's arrest. Wu was sure that his time had come. He glanced at Lieman, then averted his gaze in fear.

"What do you want?" asked Cui.

Lieman glowered at him.

"We have an announcement to make." He gestured toward the seats. "Sit down, everybody."

With pounding hearts, everyone obeyed. Wu crouched down in a chair behind broad-shouldered Mr. Mu from the Modern History Department.

"Was everyone at the assembly just now?" demanded Lieman.

No one dared to answer. Lieman turned to Cui to indicate that the question was directed at him.

"Who could stay away?" Cui observed dryly.

Sensing the defiance in Cui's reply, Lieman bristled,

but then he reminded himself that Cui was not easily intimidated. Besides, he had no evidence against Cui. He would have to be polite. Choking down his rage, he stood in silence for a moment.

"We're here for a specific reason," he growled. "Your department is harboring a criminal. I don't want to go into the nature of his crime right now. The point is, he's very sneaky. He's still at large, and he's watching our every move to see whether we know about him. I'm not going to mince words here: I've got evidence of his offense in my possession."

I'm done for, thought Wu, and he began to wait for Lieman to call his name. He rubbed his knees, smearing his trousers with sweat from his palms. This detail did not escape Lieman's eagle eye.

"I was going to have him arrested at the assembly," he said with a cackle. "But then I decided to give him another opportunity to turn himself in. Let me just make one thing clear, though: our policy has been stretched to the limit. Any more lenient, and we'd be rightists. [This was a dig at Cui.] The dictatorship of the proletariat is not to be taken advantage of. I'm giving you two more hours. If you don't turn yourself in, we'll hold another assembly this afternoon just to arrest you. All right, that's all I have to say." Lieman peered at Wu, who was still hunched over behind Mr. Mu. "Just to make sure you know you can't escape this time, I'll give you one more clue: you usually pass as a nice guy." He beckoned to Zhao, and together they swept out of the room.

Sensing that all eyes were upon him, Wu kept his head bowed. The room was whirling around him; he was blacking out. Like a drunk trying to keep his balance, he clutched the table beside him.

In the hall Lieman turned to Zhao.

"All right, let's go back and wait. He'll turn up before long."

The door clicked and Cui came running up to them from behind.

"Comrade Lieman!"

"What?" Lieman stopped and turned to Cui.

"I don't like your approach!" exclaimed Cui. "You're creating 'white terror.'[8] That's against Party policy."

Lieman arched his long thin brows. "Whom are you defending? Don't you know this is class struggle? Have you any objections?" His tone was menacing.

"Even in class struggle you can't use phony scare tactics like this. You're frightening people out of their wits."

"I think there's something wrong with your attitude, Comrade Cui. Think what you're saying! Whose ends does it serve? What do you mean, 'frightening people out of their wits'? The offenders will be frightened, but that's what a campaign is for, isn't it? I'm surprised at you. After all these years and the number of campaigns you've been through, you still don't know the first thing about class struggle."

Cui was provoked to a rare display of anger. His hands and chin trembled, and his spectacles flashed in the light that came from the small door at the end of the hall. He stood stock-still for a full ten seconds, then turned and strode away.

"I'm going to the leadership about this. This is leftism! Extreme leftism!" he said.

"Wait a minute, Cui, hold it!" Zhao moved to stop him.

Lieman grabbed Zhao by the arm.

"Let him go—don't pay any attention to him. The leadership won't back him up. They wouldn't dare stand in the way of a campaign. He's just wasting his time. Anyway, I'll get even with him later, after I've nabbed Wu."

At eleven o'clock that morning Wu trudged dejectedly up the tall, clean, cement staircase to the third floor of the rear building.

Silence reigned there. Six or seven identical little doors lined the south side of the wide corridor. Ordinarily these rooms served not as offices but as locked storerooms for valuable out-of-print rare editions, old periodicals, damaged office furniture, holiday paraphernalia (lanterns, colored flags, portraits), outsized antiques, and dusty odds and ends. Two of the rooms had once been used as dormitories for single employees from out of town, who were now all married or back in their hometowns. Long before the beginning of the Cultural Revolution the rooms had fallen into disuse. They were empty save for a few beds, washstands, cast-off shoes and socks, and shiny, crooked clothesline wires.

Hardly anyone ever came here, except during the hottest days of summer, when some of the commuters would come up and spread out a newspaper for a nap in the quiet, breezy corridor.

But a few days before, a small room at the western end of the corridor had been cleared out. A huge double-locked file cabinet, four desks, and some chairs had been moved in, and it had become the work team office. The atmosphere of the third floor was entirely transformed.

After two hours of intense mental debate, Wu had broken down completely. He was now convinced that his lost letter had fallen into Lieman's hands. He recognized his wishful thinking for what it was. There was no escaping his fate. Lieman's threats had been the coup de grace. He had come to confess.

He hesitated outside the closed office door. Twice he lifted an icy hand without knocking.

Inside, Lieman and Zhao were expecting him, as though they had exploded a depth charge underwater and were waiting for the fish to float to the surface, belly-up.

Lieman heard a rustling outside the door. His eyes glowed in their shriveled sockets. He waited, but nothing happened. It looked as if the person outside was unable to bring himself to take the fatal step.

He turned to Zhao and announced loudly:

"If he doesn't come and confess soon, I'll call an assembly for this afternoon."

There was a rapping at the door.

"Come in," Lieman answered, prompt as an angler who jerks his rod out of the water when he sees his float bobbing.

The doorknob turned; the door opened. Wu, his face ashen, entered the room and stood before Lieman's desk.

"What do you want?" snarled Lieman.

"I—I—" The words died on his lips. "I've come to report my thoughts."

"Oh?" Lieman glanced at him. "Go ahead!"

"I—uh—I've committed ideological crimes," he began, wringing his hands.

"Like what?"

"Not recently. Before—when I was in college—when I was young and immature. For example, I didn't think the state system—I didn't think our state system was perfect—and I—" he stammered. He had not planned to say this, and he had the feeling that he was digging himself in deeper with every word.

Lieman impatiently motioned for him to stop.

"Just what do you think you're doing?" he snapped. "Are you trying to test us? Look, we've known about you for ages. You're the person I was talking about a little while ago in your department office. But you're still trying to pull the wool over our eyes. You have a lot of nerve coming to the work team to try to sound us out. You're just asking for severe punishment—you're a wolf in sheep's clothing. I haven't got all day. If you have something to say, you can tell it to Zhao."

He rose and stalked out the door. As he left he signaled to Zhao behind Wu's back. His eyes said: put the screws to him.

Wu was alone in the room with his old friend Zhao.

Zhao hospitably waved a pudgy hand for him to take a seat, just as he always did when they were together. Wu, as sensitive to warmth as a man with frostbite, burst into tears.

"I wish I were dead!" he sobbed.

Zhao was stabbed by guilt. He now had ample evidence that Wu had not betrayed him. Wu's abnormal behavior had been merely a symptom of paranoia. He regretted having brought Wu to this sorry pass. Now Wu would be destroyed as soon as he confessed to anything, even if it were just some taboo remark. He noticed Wu's tear-stained, grimy cheeks. Remembering how kind and generous Wu had been to him over the years, he felt wicked. But just as he was about to comfort Wu, it struck him that Lieman was probably eavesdropping. He restrained himself. There was no turning back now.

"Come on, pull yourself together," he said. "What on earth has gotten into you? If you confess, I'm sure nothing will happen to you."

In his isolation Wu placed all his trust in his old friend.

"Zhao," he pleaded, "can you tell me whether Lieman already knows anything about me?"

Zhao wavered, then glanced warily at the closed door.

"To tell you the truth," he answered, deliberately raising his voice, "Lieman knows all about you. Don't you know you'll get off easy if you confess of your own free will?"

Tears of gratitude welled in Wu's eyes and slithered down his cheeks onto the floor.

"All right," he said. "I'll own up."

At that moment the door opened. Cigarette in hand, Lieman entered the room, followed by the cloud of smoke that had collected where he had been standing outside the door. Zhao thanked his lucky stars that he had kept his wits about him.

"Wu has come round now. He's ready to talk," Zhao announced, as if interceding for Wu.

Wu jumped to his feet, but Lieman motioned for him to be seated. Then Lieman sat down at his desk, squinting into the smoke of the cigarette dangling from his lips. With both hands he opened a drawer, took out a thick dossier, and began to leaf through it.

"Go ahead," he commanded, without so much as a glance at Wu. "Zhao, you take notes."

"Comrade Lieman, I've always done my best here at the institute!" sobbed Wu.

"Forget that for now. Get to the point," said Lieman icily, shaking his head.

As though leaping from a cliff, Wu launched recklessly into his story. As Zhao's ballpoint pen scratched across his paper, a look of shock kept flitting over his face. Lieman kept smoking his cigarette and riffling through the dossier as though he knew Wu's story already. Whenever Wu faltered, Lieman would sneer at him to keep the confession coming. Wu told about the discussion that had taken place a dozen years before at Chen Naizhi's house, holding back only with regard to his brother's role, and concluded by mentioning the lost letter.

"I simply can't find it. Honestly!"

Lieman stopped riffling through the dossier and peered at him. Zhao opened his mouth to speak, but Lieman stopped him. "Let him speak for himself."

"I took it with me that morning. I put it in my jacket pocket. But when I got to the mailbox, it was gone. I'm sure I lost it in the street."

Lieman puffed thoughtfully on his cigarette for a moment, then looked straight at Wu.

"And you think that somebody found it and delivered it to me, don't you?"

"Yes, because it was on institute stationery. I'm sure anyone who found it would bring it here."

Lieman snapped the dossier shut.

"Well, you're right," he gloated. "I've got it right here. But that's not all. That man Chen also sent us a report about you. Everything's in this dossier." He patted the thick folder. "Well, do you want to see the letter you lost?"

Wu declined with a timid shake of his head.

Wu was a ruined man, thought Zhao. He would have to dig a wide moat between himself and his unfortunate friend.

Time passed quickly. Soon the bell rang for lunch,

and Wu, whose mouth was parched from talking, asked for a drink of water. Lieman smugly locked the dossier in a drawer, as if it were a treasure.

"Well, that's not bad for a start," he said, rising. "Even though you turned yourself in under pressure, we still recognize your confession as voluntary. But you've just started to scratch the surface this morning. You haven't begun to exhaust all the information we have about you. What I want you to do now is to write up everything you've just told me. Don't try to apologize for yourself; just stick to the facts. I want separate reports about you and your brother, Chen Naizhi, and whoever else. Write everything out clearly: one, two, three, time, place, who was present, who committed what indiscretions. And rewrite the letter you lost—as a test of whether you're telling the truth. All right! Go to the empty Local History Department office and start writing. Someone will bring you your lunch."

Wu was confronted with a stack of blank paper. He felt that it was going to devour him.

As he read Wu's reproduction of the lost letter, Lieman affected nonchalance, as if he had seen the original dozens of times. But now and then his eyes glowed almost imperceptibly.

"Would you say that you've made a clean breast of things?" he asked, laying the letter on the desk.

"Yes. I was afraid to leave anything out because I knew you could compare it with the original."

Lieman nodded in satisfaction. Picking up the letter,

he put it into the drawer along with Wu's dozen-page confession. He was elated, like a hunter stuffing a newly caught rabbit into his backpack.

The work team met that afternoon. Wu was sent back to the Local History Department office to continue writing his confession.

He sat at his own desk, alone in the tranquil room. He felt as if he had returned to the peaceful routine of his old work. The feeble rays of the early afternoon sun warmed his face. On his desk were piles of books filled with note cards for his precious research project. But he had forfeited all this. Now he was doomed to endless abuse, interrogations, investigations, and an inhuman existence without dignity or freedom.

He thought of his girlfriend. Although he had not seen her since their misunderstanding of a few days before, he had a premonition of what must happen. Twice he had decided to call on her to give her a veiled account of his problem or to break up with her on some pretext. Yet he had not been able to bring himself to destroy such a rare and beautiful thing as their relationship. But now the time had come. His past was like a dead tree trunk that could no longer support buds, blossoms, leaves, or fruit.

At about four o'clock he glanced out the window and saw several people posting signs in the courtyard. His eyes widened as he caught sight of the bold lettering: "SEIZE THE ESCAPED RIGHTIST AND ACTIVE COUNTERREVO-LUTIONARY WU ZHONGYI!" His ears began to ring; his knees turned to jelly; his hands and feet went numb. He had foreseen this, yet now that it had happened he was stunned.

Within half an hour nearly all the posters in the yard referred to him. A crowd was gathering.

Again his thoughts turned to his girlfriend. He must break off their doomed relationship. He paused, then ran to the door and peeked outside. The hall was empty. Darting back into the room, he summoned up courage that had lain dormant for a dozen years. He picked up the telephone and dialed the library. She answered right away. How could such an unfortunate task go so smoothly, he wondered.

"This is Wu Zhongyi."

"What do you want?" The voice at his ear was cold. She was clearly still angry at him.

There was no need for him to apologize now.

"Come to the gate of my institute today when you get off work. I'll be waiting for you. You must come; I have something very important to tell you. Very important, do you hear? You simply must come!"

This peremptory tone was new to him. And for fear that someone might come in he hung up without waiting for her reply, although he could still hear a squawking in the receiver as he replaced it:

"What's going on? Oh—"

When the workday ended half an hour later he peeked out the window from behind the curtain. People were on their way home. Some were walking their bicycles.

A few had stopped in the yard to read the new big-character posters about him. He thought they looked shocked.

Suddenly he caught sight of a woman standing outside the main gate. On her head was a lavender gauze kerchief, and in her hand was a shiny little black purse. It was she. The stream of homebound employees was coming directly at her, and she was craning her neck to see around them into the courtyard.

Wu felt a pang of regret. Then he saw her gape in shock and draw herself bolt upright—she had discovered the posters. The passersby were looking at her inquisitively. She turned and hurried away, head bowed. Her little black purse swung rapidly as she walked.

Wu watched her disappear from sight.

He had extinguished the last light in his life.

A few days before, he had naively deluded himself that all this was just a nightmare that would vanish once he awoke. But reality had closed in on him now. The only illusion he still clung to was that the devastation could be postponed.

A brutish middle-aged man with a crew cut and beady eyes barged into the room. He was Chen Gangquan, a bachelor who doubled as a warehouseman and a worker in the maintenance and food service. Despite his boorishness, he had always been polite to Wu. During the armed struggle between the two factions, he had earned the nickname "Daredevil Chen" by leading the "Dare-to-Die Brigade" of Lieman and Zhao's faction. Now he

was warden of the detention block. He had unconsciously adopted a ruthless expression to go with his
job.

"Comrade Lieman says you can't go home anymore,"
he snarled. "He turned you over to me. Now get a
move on!"

Wu was now at his mercy. Five minutes later he
found himself sitting beside Qin.

Now he could relax. He had been floundering like a
bird in a hurricane, but now he had hit rock bottom.
He no longer had anything to fear.

But it was a dog's life in the detention block. He was
forever being hustled in and out, ordered around, and
abused. He was forbidden to talk back, and losing his
temper only earned him harsher reprimands.

Chen Gangquan was a sadist. On one occasion when
Wu unwittingly offended him, he punched Wu in the
hand, knocking his left ring finger out of joint. Even
after the swelling went down the finger remained
crooked. Wu would never forget the incident as long
as he lived. To survive in the detention block, you had
to be meek: Zhang had fared quite well there.

Wu should have been able to stay out of trouble too.
But he suffered terribly, largely because he stubbornly
tried to protect his brother. But this was easier said than
done. In the first place, his case was inseparable from his
brother's. Once they read his letter, they asked about his
brother's, and he had no choice but to tell. In the second
place, the more he held back, the more varied, cruel,

and unusual were Lieman's methods of making him talk. Lieman's overpowering tactics of psychological warfare drove him cringing from one redoubt after another. Finally he broke down and confessed all about the study group that his brother, Chen Naizhi, and the others had organized, and what his brother had said that night at Chen's house.

Two months of relative peace and quiet ensued. Except for the institute assemblies, when he, Qin, and the others were dragged out to be denounced, he was usually left alone. The work team had probably sent someone to the workplaces of his brother and Chen Naizhi to corroborate his confession. During this period he never saw Zhao.

One day while he was sweeping the courtyard, he caught sight of Zhao. His face was thinner and brown as an earthenware jar. Soon afterward, Wu was subjected to another series of tempestuous attacks. For days on end he was summoned for interrogations, which sometimes lasted into the small hours of the morning. To increase the pressure, they also staged big rallies to criticize him publicly. They wore him out.

Then Lieman confronted him with a big sheaf of materials, all denunciations of him sent in by the members of the original study group. They had paid him back in kind for his betrayal. Each of their reports was over five pages long, and Chen Naizhi had sent a fourteen-page report of Wu's criticisms of the state system. Obviously some of the contents had been fabricated in revenge. But with the passage of time he had forgotten exactly what he had said. All he could do was sign and fingerprint each of the reports, admitting to their charges.

Guilt overcame him after he succumbed to the pressure to inform on his brother. When he thought of how his betrayal would renew the suffering of his brother's family, he wished he could commit suicide. He was ashamed to be alive. Now his brother and sister-in-law would surely disown him. He was just a selfish, cowardly buffoon who lacked the courage to end his own life.

But now Lieman claimed that Wu's brother had also denounced him at length. Wu found this news oddly comforting. During interrogations Lieman never revealed the contents of his brother's report, but Wu clung to the belief that he had sent one, as if it could somehow absolve him of his heinous crime.

What on earth had become of his brother and sister-in-law?

The campaign reached a new climax in early autumn with another series of arrests. The posters in the yard proclaimed: "OPPOSE RIGHTISM!" and "GET RID OF THE STUMBLING BLOCK!" Someone was going to be attacked. Qin whispered to Wu that the target this time was Cui. One of the reasons was that Cui had allegedly treated Wu with kid gloves, which amounted to resisting the campaign and harboring a criminal. While fetching hot water in the boiler room, Qin had overheard a couple of people grumbling about the persecution of Cui. Soon a new poster mentioned Cui by name. But before the attack on Cui could get into full swing, a vice-chairman of the revolutionary committee was arrested and charged with having been the "evil patron" of the faction that had opposed Lieman. Upon his arrest he was locked up along with Qin, Wu, and the others. This incident quieted the attack on Cui.

The number of people in the detention block was growing. A room was enlarged, but it was soon crowded again. This universe, a world unto itself, seemed to be steadily devouring the one outside.

The new detainees superseded has-beens like Wu Zhongyi. Like shopworn merchandise, he was not handled without good reason. He was allowed more freedom of movement: no longer did he have to ask Chen Gangquan's permission to go to the toilet. But he was still forbidden to return home.

One day he came down with diarrhea. The work team gave him an hour to go to the infirmary, where he saw a doctor and got his medicine. Then he headed back. Late fall was in the air. Dried by the autumn wind, the leaves of the old locust tree had curled up and drifted to the ground, where they crunched underfoot. In the vast glazed blue sky, dazzling white clouds billowed like wind-filled sails. Above the gold and purple trees they added the finishing touch to the picture-perfect autumn day. The natural world seemed languid now; gone was the striving and burgeoning of summer.

Even the sun had lost its blistering heat. It now shone gently and lazily on one's face, a remarkably pleasant feeling.

Wu had been behind bars for over six months. As he walked along the street he was struck to the quick with the sweetness of life and freedom. He thought of the cluttered, dusty, long-lost apartment that he called home. Like a migrant swallow longing for its old nest, he wished he could go and take a look. But he did not dare. Although home was only a few blocks away, it might as well have been on the far side of the boundless Pacific or beyond an uncrossable mountain peak. If only he lived in a four- or five-story high rise; then at least he could glimpse the top of it from where he was standing.

He trudged on. Suddenly he felt someone blocking his way. He stopped. First he saw the feet: small and narrow, in old frayed black cloth shoes with round black leather patches on the toes. His gaze traveled slowly upward from there, finally resting on a thin, sallow, haggard female face.

"Sister-in-law!" he cried in shock.

She was wearing an old faded blue jacket, and her hair was carelessly pulled back. How well he knew those eyes! But they no longer shone with love: they were glaring at him. And he knew the reason why.

"Did you come down to see your parents? How's my brother?" he asked awkwardly.

She scowled at him instead of answering. Her tightly

compressed lips, frail shoulders—her entire body, in fact, was trembling violently with barely controlled rage. Suddenly she darted a venomous look at him, raised her hand, and gave him two resounding slaps, one on each cheek.

His face burned; his ears rang; he was blinded momentarily. He stood that way for ages, and when he came to his senses she was gone. Looking over his shoulder, he caught sight of her vanishing down the deserted sunlit street.

He stood rooted to the spot. A blue object on the ground a few yards away happened to catch his eye. Figuring that she must have dropped it, he went over to pick it up. It was her kerchief. He would never forget: a dozen years ago he had seen the same kerchief in her hair as she sat in the train window on the day when she and his two tearful little nephews went off to join his brother in exile. Blue with white dots, it was now faded, threadbare, and torn in two places. As he held it he thought of how hard her life had been and how deeply she had loved him. Her display of anger revealed what terrible suffering his betrayal had caused their whole family. His brother had finally been cleared of charges of rightism, but not before he had suffered severe facial burns while fighting a forest fire. And now he had gone and dealt him yet another blow. . . .

His eye was caught by a tiny slit of an alleyway between two nearby brick buildings: a dead end cluttered with weeds and old bricks. He darted inside, faced the wall, and began to slap his own cheeks one after the other. With each slap he sobbed and cursed himself, "You brute! Why don't you drop dead!"

He kept it up until a little girl who was passing by heard him and peered in at him curiously; then, finally, he stopped and came out onto the street, his head bowed.

That night he could not get to sleep. With swollen cheeks he lay in bed longing to find his sister-in-law, to explain to her, and to ask what had happened to his brother. He wanted to tell her that he was not entirely to blame, that it was all because he had lost a letter. That letter had cost him everything.

Lieman was back onstage. But this time his long thin face, under the visor of his green army cap, was unusually calm and friendly. The assembly was also relaxed, like a thaw after a cold winter. Wu was onstage, but no one was guarding him, and he bore no sign around his neck. His head was, however, slightly bowed.

A tempestuous six months had passed. The time had come for a general amnesty.

By the end of the previous month, thirty-seven people had been arrested at the Historical Institute. This was the fruit of almost two thousand man-hours in an organization of only one hundred members, and it was all thanks to people like Lieman.

Times had changed, and with them the slogans. The new one was: "Don't execute, imprison, or discipline unnecessarily." Now it was time for the speedy rehabilitation of all who had been arrested. Lieman now generously raised his arms to set free everyone whom he had not allowed to slip through his fingers at first.

Wu was to be released today. He was to be the first to receive a pardon.

The assembly opened routinely, with a few people coming onstage to criticize Wu for the last time. Next Lieman took the floor and read a proclamation:

"Wu Zhongyi, male, thirty-seven years of age, poor urban family. Corrupted by society from childhood, a severe case of bourgeois ideology. During the Antirightist Campaign of 1957, participated in a reactionary study group organized by brother Wu Zhongren and some others. Expressed rightist views of a serious nature. Never confessed to the Party. After beginning of present campaign, corresponded secretly with brother and plotted to continue to cover up offense and to resist the campaign. But was eventually moved by Party policy and the might of our dictatorship of the proletariat to confess voluntarily. Repeated investigations showed that confession was basically truthful. Behavior was good in reform-through-labor.

"In order to implement Party policy to the letter, in the spirit of curing the disease and saving the patient, and in consideration of Wu's good behavior, the revolutionary committee has decided, after review and approval by the higher leadership, that Wu's grave wrongdoing does not call for criminal sanctions. His is a case of contradiction among the people. Beginning today his job and salary will be restored. We hope that when Comrade Wu returns to his old post he will apply himself diligently to the study of Marxism-Leninism and Mao Zedong Thought, work hard, reform himself through practice, and turn over a new leaf."

Stunned, Wu glanced up at the faces in the audience and saw that many of them looked pleased. Then he turned to Lieman, who was also smiling, a sight rarer than a total eclipse of the moon. Now he believed that he was not dreaming. Life had returned to him all that it had snatched away. Director Hao of the revolutionary committee approached him, pinned a brass Mao button on his chest, presented him with a set of *Selected Works of Mao Zedong*, and shook his hand. A flood of warmth spread over Wu, and he jerked his arm skyward in salute.

"Long live the Great Proletarian Cultural Revolution!" he shouted, with such force that his feet seemed to leave the floor. His face was wet with tears of gratitude.

"Now listen, Wu," said Lieman, "don't imagine that you did nothing wrong. You must remember this lesson and understand the campaign. It was correct to arrest you in the first place, and it is also correct to set you free now. You must thank the Party for saving you."

Wu nodded tearfully. He believed Lieman with all his heart.

Reeling under the suddenness of his good fortune, he stepped down from the stage. Zhao, who was standing there to welcome him back in the name of the Local History Department, came forward with a friendly smile, extended his warm soft hands, and tightly clasped Wu's trembling ones.

Wu left the assembly with Zhao. All along the way people silently beamed him congratulatory smiles. Then Chen Gangquan approached them. He had been waiting to hustle Wu back to the block after the assembly but was now grinning broadly.

"Don't hold it against me, Wu," he said. "I did it for the revolution."

Wu laughed nervously and shook his head. He was not the sort to bear a grudge; all he wanted was to be forgiven.

In the hall of the front building he ran into Cui. The tall thin department chairman was aloof, as always. Wu paused, remembering the day before his arrest, when Cui had taken him into the empty Local History Department office and offered so much heartfelt advice, while he had fearfully held back his secret. And later, he recalled, during his period of ostracism, Cui had never pressured him; for this, Cui had been accused of rightism. Now, facing Cui, he felt apologetic and cast about awkwardly for something to say.

Through his square black wire-rimmed glasses Cui peered at Zhao, who was escorting Wu.

"Remember the lesson you've been taught," he said simply in a muffled voice and hurried away.

Wu would never know how violently Cui had argued with Zhao about his case.

Zhao led Wu into the Local History Department

office. As they stood before Wu's old desk, Zhao took Wu's right hand and dropped something cold and hard into it. Wu glanced down—his desk key lay glittering in his hand. He had been ordered to surrender it on the day of his arrest, and now it was being returned to him along with the work he loved.

Zhao was beaming at him, just as in the old days.

"I didn't let you come to grief, did I?" he asked.

Wu was reminded of what Zhao had said on the day of his confession in the work team office. He believed that Zhao had helped him in his moment of crisis: thanks to the advice of this dear friend he had been pardoned today. Tears welled up anew in his red-rimmed eyes. He was speechless, but his heart was bursting with gratitude.

At last he was on his way home, free as a bird released from its cage. If he just raised his arms he would soar right up into the heavens.

On the way he spent the meager sum in his pocket on a bottle of beer and some food and candy to celebrate. He had not yet touched the beer, but already he was tottering like a drunken Immortal. And his cheeks were burning, even though his head was bare in the dead of winter.

He reached his long-lost home. In the dim corridor he found his neighbor Mrs. Yang shoveling coal briquets with her little grandson.

"My goodness! Comrade Wu! You're back!" she exclaimed.

"That's right," he replied jauntily.

"You—uh—didn't—" Mrs. Yang checked herself, afraid to talk without knowing what his current status was. She stood there stiffly holding her shovel.

Wu was also tongue-tied.

Mrs. Yang laughed awkwardly.

"Why don't you go on upstairs and light the stove and get warm," she said perfunctorily. Snatching her grandson by the hand, she turned and waddled nervously inside as if he were a patient escaped from quarantine.

Wu did not take offense. He would come downstairs and explain to her later.

He opened the door and entered his room. The air was musty. His things were just as he had left them, although they looked slightly unfamiliar. The cluttered furnishings—bed, desk, chairs, cups—appeared stunned by his sudden arrival. But then, as if they had sensed their master's homecoming, they seemed to warm up to him. In return his heart went out to these lifeless companions. Then he noticed that everything was coated with dust. He circled around the room wondering where to begin cleaning. Finally he got a grip on himself and decided to light the stove first. Fortunately it was ready to use—he had been imprisoned in the springtime before dismantling it.

His heart sank as soon as he touched the ashes in the stove: the remains of the discarded letters he had burned that fateful morning. The thought of his brother and sister-in-law made him uneasy. He decided to go to his sister-in-law's parents' house that evening to find out how his brother and sister-in-law were. But how would he ever explain everything to them? At any rate, he would never write another letter as long as he lived.

His hands were grimy after he lit the stove, so he went to wash them. The washbasin was filled with dirty ice. During the days of distraction after he had lost the letter, he had hardly ever washed his face. At most he had mechanically dipped his handkerchief into the basin and dabbed at his cheeks with it. Since the water had not been changed for days, the basin-shaped piece of ice was an opaque dark gray.

Picking up the basin, he turned it over to dump the ice onto the stove. Suddenly something caught his eye: a letter was stuck to the bottom. Puzzled, he put the basin down and removed the letter. When he saw what it was his brows twitched so violently that his glasses almost slipped off. It was the lost letter, the letter that had nearly cost him his life. It was stamped and sealed: after he had finished writing it that morning he had slapped on some paste, affixed the stamp, and sealed it. Then he had placed the basin on the table to wash his face, and the excess paste on the envelope had adhered to the bottom of the wet basin. Who would have dreamed that this was where it had been all along?

"Oh!" he cried in shock and stood transfixed, like an exclamation point. By the time he had grasped all the implications, he had been standing there a full thirty minutes.

Winding Brook Way

For some reason I dislike neatly pruned trees. I prefer natural, gnarled trunks with sprawling branches and patchy, unkempt foliage. Take my hair for example. I hate to go to the barber shop and have it set and blow-dried so that it comes out looking like a shiny new black shoe. And when I go to the Summer Palace[1] I bypass Harmony Garden[2] to stroll along dirt paths in the unspoiled woods. As for the Covered Walkway[3] with its colorful paintings and fine carvings, one visit was enough for me. My friends often scoff at my taste. I don't argue with them, however, because I cannot explain myself. But I know what I like.

Once a group of foreign tourists was scheduled to visit a park famous for its trees. It was late autumn and fallen leaves lay a foot deep on the ground. There were two park superintendents, A and B. Superintendent A wanted to mobilize the entire park work force to rake up all the leaves, no mean feat in a park of more than three hundred acres.

Superintendent B was an old gardener who knew the art of landscaping. In his opinion the park looked beautiful the way it was. Fallen leaves underfoot lent the scenery a special charm. "Yellow leaves piled on the ground are worth as much as gold in a mound," he said. All the park workers agreed with him, but primarily because they were too lazy to rake the leaves.

The next day the tourists arrived. They delighted in walking on the thick, resilient carpet of rustling golden leaves. They hiked to a lake beside which were stone tables and stools, blanketed with a layer of leaves. Brushing the leaves away with his sleeve, Superintendent B told his men to set out beer and a snack. As they ate, the tourists enjoyed the gorgeous autumn scene. The fallen leaves gave off a warm fragrance in the sunlight. Transported by the sheer beauty of nature, the tourists gradually fell silent.

Superintendent A was delighted. They had gotten extraordinary results without lifting a finger. But he did not give much thought to the reason for the success.

When I heard this story I decided that the old gardener, Superintendent B, had the makings of a poet.

I live at 19 Winding Brook Way, so called because of the little brook that once meandered past my door. It was a lovely, placid brook, whose sparkling waters held reflections of the weeping willows along its banks and of the clouds, birds, and children's kites in the sky. It always flowed in silence—except for the cracking of its ice in spring, the rushing of its waters in summer, or the lapping of its waves in a storm.

The brook was only fifty or sixty paces from my door. As a child I used to play with my friends on its grassy, flowery banks, bathe in its waters, and squat beside it watching straw-hatted fishermen lift gleaming silversides swishing from the water. Once an old fisherman even let me try his fishing rod, but all I managed to hook was some waterweed. I learned to fish eventually, but my real specialty was climbing the old willow trees to rob crows' nests. Many a time I slithered nimbly down the tall black gnarled tree trunks with an armload of blue crows' eggs, savoring the admiring look on the upturned face of the girl next door.

An artist used to come here, a dark, thin, taciturn fellow with paint-splattered clothes, who rode a bicycle on which he carried a flat wooden case of twisted tubes of oil paint. The brook attracted him like a magnet: he came every day. At first he painted on the far bank, then he moved over to our side. I liked him, probably because he liked our brook.

I say "our brook" out of habit, because all the residents of Winding Brook Way spoke as if the brook rightfully belonged to us. The grown-ups strictly forbade us children to urinate in it because it was our water supply, and they used it to wash clothes, vegetables, and rice.

One day I stood watching the painter mix his colors and dab them onto his canvas, which was stretched on a wooden frame. He ignored me. He would look up at the brook, then down at his painting, and shake his head and sigh. Capturing our brook on canvas was evidently rather difficult.

"Your painting is no good," I told him.

Without lifting his eyes from the canvas, he turned his head slightly toward me.

"What's wrong with it?"

"Our brook is alive, but it looks dead in your painting," I answered bluntly, unable to explain further.

My remark seemed to hit home. He gaped at me, taken aback. Then he scraped the paint off his canvas with a wooden-handled triangular blade, banged his case shut, and rode away on his bicycle. He never came back. I was sorry that I had offended him. But when I looked at the brook my regrets vanished as if borne away on a gust of wind. Our brook was proof that I had been right: the brook itself was a beautiful work of art.

From inside the house the brook was framed in my window like a living painting that changed endlessly with the seasons, weather, and time of day. The view was ordinary—just a brook and some scraggly old willows—but it would turn golden in the glow of sunset, green in the rains of spring, white after a heavy snowfall, and blurry in a thick fog. Against this background, the tree trunks, crows' nests, and fishermen looked like dabs of ink. So I had no other decorations on my walls. The window was enough for me.

———

"Hey, Dad, look how pretty the brook is!" exclaimed my son one morning.

I was shocked by what I saw from my window. The brook had turned a purple color, clashing violently with the blue of the sky and the green of the reeds. Our brook had always been delicate, like a watercolor; never had I seen it take on such a garish hue.

Once outside, I discovered that a purple chemical solution was contaminating the brook. Glancing upstream, I saw a concrete-walled compound containing several red brick buildings and a big tall smokestack— a dye plant built the year before.

From then on there was a continuous flow of the purple liquid. The brook was no longer transformed by changes in the weather but stayed the same gaudy, forbidding shade of purple day in, day out. Whenever there was an overspill of the liquid, purple scum frothed on the banks. Like some underwater demon, it killed off the lush growth of reeds, wiped out the fish that had once rippled the water, and drove away the fishermen. When spring came, the grass on the embankments showed hardly any sign of life. Even eerier, the new leaves on the hardy old willows shriveled, fell, and lay strewn on the ghastly purple water. The crows' nests were still in the treetops, but the crows were gone. Their cawing and the croaking of frogs on a summer's evening would never be heard again.

The local people stopped using the brook as their water supply and began to dump garbage into it. During a drought that summer, the brook turned into a dry stinking ditch, where litter tumbled in the warm breeze.

I was reminded of the painter from twenty years before.

"This brook is dead anyway, isn't it?" he would have retorted if the brook had looked like this back then.

The brook was dead. No painters would return here. Painters are different from writers. A writer can be inspired by death, whereas a painter is usually moved by beautiful, natural life.

The people of Winding Brook Way began to negotiate with the dye plant and eventually took the matter to court.

One day a young woman and a middle-aged man came with pipettes and little bottles to take water samples, but they refused to answer any questions about what the samples were for. Everyone began to hope that something would be done to restore the brook to life, but six months passed and the pair did not return.

Soon afterward we heard that the dye plant had signed a contract with a nearby commune. The commune had agreed to sell the brook and several acres of land across the water from us to the dye plant as a warehouse site, in return for which the plant was to find jobs for one hundred peasants and to subcontract the painting of all its dye barrels to the commune.

This brought the matter to a speedy conclusion. People from the dye plant and the commune trooped in with carts, shovels, picks, saws, and an old bulldozer and set to work with a vengeance. First they chopped down all the trees in sight and carted them off. Next they drained the brook, sank concrete sewer pipes into the dry riverbed, and tore down the embankments. And so one little brook was removed from the face of the earth.

Then they built a big warehouse. And fifty or sixty paces from my door, where the brook had been, there was now a broad dirt road.

One day a passerby asked me, "Where's Winding Brook Way?"

"This is it," I said.

He look around and lifted his eyebrows in surprise. "But where's the brook?"

I glanced across the dusty road at the long drab wall around the warehouse, with its mountain of black dye barrels.

"The brook is gone!" I sighed.

I cannot take the clouds of dust and the constant rumble of passing trucks. Worst of all is the strange choking smell that wafts over from the dye plant whenever the wind blows from the south.

I want to move away.

But in this crowded city of buildings, smokestacks, and hubbub, is there a spot left where a person can live among trees, greenery, and flowers? Just a quiet, poetic little brook would do. . . .

Plum Blossoms in the Snow

Unlike most other park visitors, who were enjoying the scenery at a leisurely pace, I headed straight for the far right corner as fast as my legs could carry me. Taking a shortcut across a few grassy knolls, I arrived at a small, old-fashioned crimson pavilion, its courtyard tastefully planted with flowering peach trees but mobbed with people. When I saw the sign on the gate, "Paintings by the Late Shen Zhuoshi," I felt a tightening in my stomach. Nervously making my way to the gate, I bought a ticket, stuffed it into the ticket taker's hand, and entered the exhibition along with a crowd of young people in bright holiday clothes.

I found myself in a world of color, as magnificent as the glow of dawn above a river. I feasted my eyes upon flowers in full bloom under the midday sun, great rivers gleaming in the moonlight, soaring flocks of birds, torrential waterfalls spraying clouds of mist, precipitous mountain ranges towering into the heavens, green fertile fields stretching into the distance, mountain villages sleeping beneath heavy snow, willow branches dripping with raindrops, bees crawling about inside flowers, shy sparrows chirping in winter forests, sailboats in the mist, eagles wheeling in the sky . . .

The paintings greeted me warmly, like long-lost friends. I was trembling with excitement, but rather than linger over each one with the other spectators, I threaded my way through the crowd, surveying the pictures purposefully. Then the shock of recognition brought me up short. Here it was—the painting I would never forget as long as I lived.

Mounted on a scroll of plain gray damask, the three-foot-square painting hung in solemn silence and blazed with passion. A gnarled old plum tree stood its ground in a raging blizzard, lashed by ice and snow. The iron of its roots thrust deep into a cracked boulder, and its thin, stiff, forked branches reached skyward with strong, graceful tips. The tree had only a few scattered blossoms—luminous vermilion spheres. I felt as if I were looking straight into those familiar eyes—round, flashing, bloodshot—once again. The title inscribed at the top in bold characters read: *Plum Blossoms in the Snow*. The vibrant, forceful calligraphy captured the fervor of the hand that had written those words. The sight moved me to tears.

I quickly pulled out a handkerchief to dab my eyes. In the crowd around me, one boy was copying the painting onto a clipboard. He kept stealing curious glances in my direction. Other onlookers had noticed me too. I was embarrassed at my lack of self-restraint, yet these people had no idea of the suffering that lay behind this painting. How I wished I could tell them about the artistic integrity embodied here. . . .

It all began during a cold snap one winter. The sky was leaden, but there was no snow. Even when the wind would drop momentarily, the air was so frigid and dry you felt as if your face would crack. It was one of the worst winters in years.

I was on the faculty of the Print Department of the Art Institute, but I seldom taught, because of a heart condition. One evening just before dinner a colleague came by with distressing news: Lao Shen, a professor in the Traditional Chinese Painting Department, had been singled out again for severe criticism at a schoolwide faculty and staff meeting held that day.

Earlier in the year, Lao Shen had been one of a dozen artists invited to decorate the lobby of the newly built Friendship Hotel. He had painted some innovative landscapes and flower-and-bird scenes. Two days before, the Municipal Party Secretary of Culture and Education, Zhao Xiong, had gone to inspect the paintings. Lao Shen's work had sent him into a towering rage. He claimed it contained "arrows tipped with anti-Party poison." Although no evidence against Lao Shen had been presented at the meeting that day, everyone in the audience sensed that he was a marked man. Lao Shen sat in back, so that my colleague, seated up front, had been unable to observe his reactions.

My colleague's visit was short. When he rose to take his leave, I escorted him part of the way.

"Why on earth did Lao Shen bother?" he said, shaking his head. "He knew perfectly well that Zhao was going to inspect the paintings and that Zhao is a professional nitpicker who knows nothing about painting. What's more, he knows that Zhao doesn't like him. So why did he try to be creative? He'd have done better just to splash bright red and green paint all over the canvas and be done with it. Why fuss over composition, technique, and brushstrokes? This is no time to try to be artistic—it's hard enough just to keep your head attached to your shoulders these days. Why stick your neck out? Lao Shen is much too stubborn—he's suffered tremendously over the last few years, but he just won't give in. Really—"

That outburst was a bad omen for Lao Shen, I thought, but I held my tongue. Over the past several years I had trained myself to conform for safety's sake and had learned to keep quiet whenever I disagreed with anyone except a close friend. In silence I saw my colleague off. Returning to my room, I sat down at the table and picked up my bowl but simply could not eat.

Over twenty years before, Lao Shen and I, along with another professor of traditional Chinese painting named Pan Danian, had been classmates at the National Art Institute in Beijing. At first Lao Shen and I studied Western painting together; we liked each other and soon became fast friends. We had great expectations then—for us the future was a vast clean canvas waiting to be filled in with a misty rainbow of colors.

Since Lao Shen was an outspoken radical, the school authorities kept him under surveillance as a Red. He was a hard worker. I remember that during the two years that he and I were in the same class he gradually filled the space under his bed with drawings. His talent and honesty earned him the esteem of his fellow students.

Lao Shen had originally planned a career as a painter in oils, but as foreign aggression mounted, patriots began boycotting foreign goods. So he abandoned Western painting, in which he was already highly accomplished, and took up traditional Chinese watercolor. He joined Pan Danian's class, and the two became friends.

After liberation the three of us, laden with bundles, easels, and wicker trunks, came to teach at this institute. Lao Shen and Pan joined the Traditional Chinese Painting Department, while I taught drawing in the Print Department. By dint of hard work and sheer talent, Lao Shen gradually surpassed the two of us and became a famous painter. He was also known for the effectiveness of his teaching and had many students, a number of whom achieved some renown themselves. He was promoted to lecturer, then to assistant professor, full professor, and department chairman. Even after the three of us got married, we remained close friends.

Lao Shen was a rock, but the friction of life had given him rough edges rather than polishing him smooth. However skillfully he had learned to handle a paintbrush, socially he was as naive as a teenager. He was out-spoken to the point of being refractory and always protested against scandal or injustice, even at the cost of embarrassing his superiors. Bullies feared him. But he was the hero of all underdogs, many of whom tried unsuccessfully to imitate him. People said he was "defiant."

"Where did they get that idea?" he would ask, a smile playing about his tobacco-stained lips. "It's just that I'm not a pushover. Anyway, if you're too weak, you bend with every breeze and crumble under the slightest pressure."

I was usually less hotheaded than Lao Shen and sel-dom clashed with anyone. But when it came to art, I was just as serious and intolerant—even argumentative—as he. Of course in later years when private opinions were proscribed, I learned to modify such dangerous personality traits. In our student days, however, Lao Shen and I could argue about art till we were both red in the face. (Thinking back, I was the conservative and he the innovator.) Even though this was only intellectual sparring, our pride often led us to part in anger. And since we were also in different departments, Pan grad-ually replaced me as Lao Shen's best friend. Pan was a more mild-mannered, close-mouthed man, not the type to joust over opinions. But my friendly feelings and professional admiration for Lao Shen were not affected by our altercations. Such little pebbles could never have filled the deep lake of our long-standing friendship.

When the Cultural Revolution began, all three of us

were attacked. We were even locked up together in one of the makeshift prisons people in those days called "cow sheds."

Since Lao Shen was department chairman and a famous artist, he was a more conspicuous target for the student radicals than Pan or I. He was the first to come under fire. His house was searched and his living quarters reduced in size. As his old friends, Pan and I were considered guilty by association. At every mass rally, Lao Shen was led on stage first, followed by Pan and me. Eventually we were all sent off to farms for "reeducation" through manual labor.

When classes resumed, Pan was the first to be reinstated at school. Thanks to his usual circumspection, the charges against him had been the least serious. Half a year later Lao Shen was also transferred back. Prominent men like him were not permitted quiet, uneventful lives but were constantly shunted about with every change in political policy.

My case was different. I was a lower-echelon teacher with a questionable family background, who was not missed at the institute. After three years in the fields I was finally transferred back, thanks to petitions submitted by Lao Shen and others to the head of the institute. But soon after I returned to teaching my heart trouble started, and I had to convalesce at home. I seldom went out except for occasional visits to Lao Shen.

Lao Shen's ordeal had little visible effect on him; he continued to devote himself single-mindedly to his teaching and research. Since art was inseparable from politics in those days, most artists learned to keep their opinions to themselves. But Lao Shen, like an alien just dropped to Earth from outer space, continued to be passionately creative. When talking about art he would pace back and forth like a victorious general expatiating on his troops. I had never seen him so intense; his defiance seemed deliberate. His lack of circumspection worried me, and I tried to scare some sense into him.

"Don't you know that they can take any innocent remark as an excuse to charge you with any crime they want? Haven't you suffered enough? Are you crazy? Can't you just keep your mouth shut?" I stopped short when I saw the stubborn challenging glint and veiled look of contempt in his big dark eyes.

"No, I can't," he said, motioning to me to be quiet.

I hung my head in silence. He wasn't being rude. I understood him. Laymen can hardly grasp what art means to a real artist. But I could, because I had once been like him—although I had abandoned my principles or, rather, hidden them away.

I knew he was courting danger. He was a bird soaring about boldly while bullets whizzed by him on all sides. But all I could do was wait.

And now disaster had struck. How was he doing?

Leaving my dinner untouched, I grabbed a warm hat and set off for his house.

I found him alone, sitting at a battered little round table and drinking gloomily out of a small hexagonal white porcelain cup. Instead of rising to greet me, he used a thrust of his stubbly sharp chin to motion for me to sit down across from him. Then he stood up and brought me a pair of cheap wooden chopsticks and a cup to match his. He pointed with his chopsticks to the food on the table, indicating that I should help myself.

There were a few plates, each with a small helping of food: fried peanuts, smoked bean curd, salted fish, cabbage salad. There was also a bamboo basket of pancakes covered with a yellowish cloth. In the middle of the table lay a dozen large dried red peppers—Lao Shen was from Sichuan.

He went on drinking and made no show of politeness. I had dropped in and found him drinking many times before, but tonight the atmosphere was unusually gloomy. Lao Shen did not seem himself at all. Usually he would urge liquor on me while loudly holding forth on the topic of his choice. Even the pressures of the last two years had not quieted him down. But tonight he just drank morosely and chewed on a pepper that looked so hot it scared me.

He was wearing a close-fitting padded jacket of black satin. Lao Shen was a thin man; the bulge at his belly was a dark green hot-water bottle. He had both a stomach ailment and high blood pressure, and they had aged him prematurely. His graying hair was combed back like an old man's, but unruly locks stuck out all over. Like a rambunctious boy, he hated to go to the barber, and his hair hung down over his ears and collar. He habitually pushed it out of his face with the splayed fingers of his left hand—there was always a paintbrush in his right. But the hair was as insubordinate as the man and would fall loose again the moment he moved his head. He was balding at the temples, and his large smooth forehead was a globe traversed by mountains and rivers of blue veins. When he was excited—happy or angry—the veins bulged. They were bulging now, and he was scowling.

Like strangers sharing a table in a bar, we drank in gloomy silence.

On the small iron stove behind him was a kettle. It had long since come to a boil, and the lid was clattering. Soft regular snores came from the other side of an old blue door curtain, where Mrs. Shen was asleep in the bedroom. She, too, was in poor health and still childless after sixteen or seventeen years of marriage. When Lao Shen met with adversity in his work, his homelife provided no comfort.

His reduced living quarters were the size of an efficiency apartment, although there was a separate bedroom barely large enough for a double bed. The outer room, which served as both living and dining room, was also Lao Shen's studio. Sketches and drafts were tacked up all over the walls; in some spots they were layered on top of each other. Along the walls were two clotheslines onto which more paintings were pinned like laundry. In one corner was a draftsman's table; half of it was piled with books and albums, the other half covered with a felt blotter. On the front edge was a jumble of ink stones, water basins, paint jars, and stamp pads. On the wall hung two chopsticks baskets—one contained chopsticks, the other an assortment of brushes. There was also a peg above the table from which he could hang the ceiling light and work at night instead of sleeping.

I sat staring at the veins bulging on his forehead. I wanted to speak but was afraid to disturb him.

"Won't you try these hot peppers?" he asked suddenly. "They won't kill you. What are you afraid of?" Fixing his dark eyes on me, he raised his neat heavy eyebrows, which looked as though he had painted them on. His face and voice betrayed deep emotion.

I paused for a moment. "You Sichuanese are used to spicy food. But I don't see how you can swallow it when it's so hot," I suggested.

Lao Shen looked displeased. But instead of arguing, he lifted his drink and downed half of it in one gulp. He hung his head for a moment, then looked up and drained his cup. Next he began to chew on a finger-sized pepper, smiling at me as he did so. He looked defiant and obstinate, and bursting with drunken energy.

He rose and went wordlessly to his table, spread a snowy sheet of paper on the felt blotter, ground some ink, and took out a scruffy long-tipped weasel-hair paintbrush. Seeing that he was going to paint, I brought the light over for him and fastened it onto the peg.

Brush in hand, Lao Shen stared at the smooth white paper for a moment. His eyebrows fluttered excitedly, like the wings of a startled swallow. His emotion then flowed into his brush, which began to tremble wildly. He lifted his elbow, and the inky brush swooped down onto the paper like a sparrow hawk onto a rabbit. It dabbed and swept the paper, as if it were a willow branch brushing the surface of water in a gale. The black shape that appeared on the white paper was unidentifiable, but not for long. Soon it was clearly a hardy old plum tree.

Lao Shen swirled the brush in a basin, and the ink clouded the water. Next he dipped the brush twice in powder and returned it quivering to the paper, across which it boldly splattered water, ink, and powder. And a raging blizzard spread over the sky. Lao Shen's brush had captured winter's forbidding cold on the paper. Now the plum branches looked even hardier.

He painted with his whole body, propping his left hand on the table as if to keep himself from pouncing onto the painting. Two locks of hair had fallen onto his forehead. He let them swing there like tassels. The only sounds in the room were the scratch of the brush across the paper and the clink of the brush handle against the water basin and paint dishes. Out of a corner of my eye I noticed his mouth twitching—from exertion, the unchewed red pepper in his mouth, or anguish? The veins on his temples were swollen and purplish.

The door opened and in came Pan, accompanied by a young woman named Fan Ying, a former student of Lao Shen, but now his colleague. I nodded to them, indicating with my glance that they should not disturb Lao Shen. They nodded, quietly removed their winter wraps, and stood behind him to watch him paint. Although he seemed aware of their presence, he did not wrench himself from his trance to greet them. They looked grave at first, but they quickly responded to the painting's message. Fan's pretty eyes glistened with tears, while Pan shook his head and sighed softly with deep emotion.

When Lao Shen had finished with the ink, he took a large, clean, goat-hair brush, dipped it into a dish of carmine paint, and added a handful of brilliant flowers to the tree. A proud, fearless plum tree now braved the elements. There was nothing gentle about it; the tree was a hero in adversity. Then Lao Shen dabbed the dry weasel-hair brush into the ink again and inscribed the title at the top: *Plum Blossoms in the Snow*. The calligraphy was dignified and calm, firm and bold, as solid as cast iron. It suited the painting perfectly.

He signed his work, checked it over quickly, added a few finishing touches, and threw his brush down on the table. He turned to look at Fan and Pan, then at me, and parted his tobacco-stained lips in a grin. Bits of red pepper clung to his teeth. His eyes were flashing. The painting was his wordless response to my oblique question and to all of our concern.

We were all touched to the quick. Never, in all my years as an artist, had a painting ever had such an effect on me, though, of course, the reason was in part extrinsic to the painting itself.

"Lao Shen," Pan exclaimed, "your painting is a great comfort. It says all there is to say."

The rims of Lao Shen's eyes reddened, but he bit his lip as if to control his feelings.

"I have a request," continued Pan earnestly.

"What?"

"May I have this painting? It represents you—no, it *is* you! I can't tell you how wonderful it is. Yang Wujiu, Wang Mian, Jin Dongxin,[1] and Lao Fou[2] were all great, but this is more heroic than anything of theirs. No, it's more than heroic, it—" Pan fell silent; he was tongue-tied.

Nothing is more comforting and satisfying to an artist than friendship and true appreciation. Lao Shen pushed his hair out of his face; he had brightened considerably since my arrival.

"All right," he answered without a moment's hesitation. He stamped the painting with his seal, rolled it up, and presented it to Pan. I remember that I felt vaguely uneasy as I watched Pan accept it. But before I could analyze these feelings there was a knock at the door. Fan answered it. In the doorway stood half a dozen young people—Lao Shen's students. Like us, they were worried about the reports that Lao Shen had been criticized. I was touched by their concern.

Lao Shen was naturally even more moved than I. Arms wide, he beckoned to them to come in—he always greeted students affectionately. Once they were inside he bustled around finding them seats and pouring water. The students were surprised at his manner at first but then burst into relieved laughter. They knew how tough and optimistic their teacher was and had hoped that this would be his reaction.

The room was crowded. I took my leave of Lao Shen,

and Fan rose to go with me. But Pan had disappeared. Eventually we found him skulking outside the door, his face bundled up in a face mask and scarf. He was apparently afraid his reputation would suffer if word got out that he had visited Lao Shen.

Lao Shen escorted us to the gate.

"Professor Shen," Fan said anxiously, "don't you think you should withdraw your painting from the Municipal Art Show?"

"Why?"

"I'm sure Zhao Xiong is going to inspect the paintings there. He's already out to get you. Don't give him anything else to use against you."

"No," countered Lao Shen. "He won't be able to find anything wrong with my painting. Don't worry about him."

"I think you should withdraw too," said Pan. "Some of these people are terrible hairsplitters. Why not try to stay out of trouble for once?"

"Well, just let him try to find something wrong with it," said Lao Shen with a laugh. "It would offer me a rare learning experience."

He was intransigent, although clearly aware of the danger. He is definitely headed for trouble, I thought. How could an artist armed with nothing but a paintbrush do battle with a mighty VIP? I could not understand how an intelligent man like Lao Shen could be so obstinate. But before I could say anything he waved to us, turned, and went back inside the gate.

As we walked, the three of us discussed how to persuade Lao Shen to withdraw his painting from the show. When we parted I felt the same vague uneasiness again, but this time I managed to put my finger on it.

"Pan," I said, "be sure to put Lao Shen's painting away. Be careful whom you show it to."

Pan shook his head and smiled. "What do you think I am, a three-year-old?"

Relieved by his answer, I turned home, my step lighter than when I had left.

Ten days later my department sent me an invitation to the preview of the Municipal Art Show that same afternoon. The person who brought the invitation told me that Secretary Zhao would probably use the occasion to inspect the paintings. I left at once for the show. Frankly, art shows in those days didn't interest me much. The only reason for my going to this one was that I was worried about Lao Shen. Fan had told me two days before that she had tried again to persuade him to withdraw his painting from the show and that he had again refused.

Everyone knew that Zhao, former chief of the Bureau of Commerce, had had a meteoric rise during the last two years. Although he was in charge of culture, he was an ignoramus when it came to art. His tyranny had earned him the hatred of writers and artists. The absurd, private jokes that circulated about him would make a hilarious comedy routine nowadays. The first time he went to inspect an art show—which may also have been the first time he had ever been to one in his life—he said, "I really don't get it—what's the use of all these pictures?"

The sad thing was that he determined the fate of works of art. And in those days the fate of a work of art was a matter of life and death for the artist. So Zhao's inspections were trials both for artists and their works. If he had any special talent, it was the ability to find heinous crimes in perfectly ordinary paintings. Fear of him kept many people—like myself—from entering art shows. Now that Lao Shen had been singled out by Zhao, he was almost certainly headed for more trouble.

At the exhibition hall I was greeted by a slender, pretty young woman wearing a triangular, tan mohair stole that nicely offset her rosy cheeks. It was Fan.

"Is Lao Shen here?" I asked, stepping forward to greet her.

"Not yet, but he should be here any minute."

"Do you have a painting on exhibit?"

"Yes." She lowered her gaze modestly, her long, even lashes covering her sparkling eyes. "It's over there. Please come and see it—I'd appreciate any suggestions you might have."

The painting, entitled *By the Fields*, was an ingenious composition in the traditional, realistic style. It depicted a grassy flowery slope at the edge of a field. On the slope was a still life: a big earthenware jug of drinking water, some sparkling enamel mugs, a few towels, and a couple of jackets with a plastic notebook and a rolled-up newspaper sticking out of the pockets. There was also a transistor radio. The objects had clearly been left there

by the farmers, and they intrigued the viewer by remind-
ing him of the absent owners. I admired both the artist's
powers of observation and her ability to capture a scene.
The fresh, pretty clusters of flowers—all wildflowers
I could not identify—gave life to the painting, for they
had been drawn from life, not just copied from a textbook. I offered my sincerest compliments. But she would
not take credit for the achievement.

"Professor Shen took me out on several field trips so
that I could sketch for this painting. He wouldn't let me
copy textbooks or magazines. He told me, 'Your feelings are the wellspring of your creativity, and you won't
have any real feelings unless you paint from life. Paintings without feeling lack the power to move people.
Life is the ultimate textbook, and only a fool throws
that away and confines himself to the thin, lifeless,
ready-made books of others.' You see what interesting
things he says—" She crinkled her eyes in a smile filled
with respect for her teacher.

That sounded like Lao Shen all right. In "reeducation" school in the countryside, whenever he discovered
an unusual wildflower in the fields during the day, he
would hurry back to sketch it when the day's work
was done. He would draw in the golden light of sunset
and not quit until his easel was enveloped in darkness.
He was fascinated by unfamiliar plants and would often
pick samples so that he could ask the old peasants about
them. For this he was accused of "not wholeheartedly
devoting himself to thought reform." But he turned a
deaf ear to such scandalmongering. Whenever he re-

turned home on vacation he would spend hours reading botanical textbooks at the library. And now his ideas were influencing the next generation.

The relationship Lao Shen had established between himself and his student Fan was widely admired. When Lao Shen returned from "reeducation" he was no longer department chairman—the position had been abolished. He was vice-group leader. Following orders from higher up, the revolutionary committee of the institute appointed Fan, a recent institute graduate, group leader. This fashionable personnel arrangement was a patent expression of distrust of Lao Shen. The idea was to use easily controlled young people like Fan to supervise their elders. The usual result of this policy was a clash between the generations. People predicted that Lao Shen and Fan would quarrel. But as far as I know, they got along beautifully.

Fan was a decent young woman, not the sort to step on others to advance her own career. Nor was she arrogant or overly pragmatic like so many young people in those days. She respected Lao Shen and studied diligently. Because the two of them had a great deal in common, they became close friends. Lao Shen never stinted to teach her everything he knew. And with his perceptive eye he recognized that just as Fan herself was gentle and quiet, her painting style was delicate, unlike his own. He was not the kind of teacher who rides roughshod over a student's individuality, forcing him or her to follow in his own footsteps. His task, as he saw it, was to enable students to develop their own styles. He helped Fan to find a neat, attractive style of her own. As a result she had already made a name for herself as a promising young artist. I liked Fan too. Nothing makes a teacher happier than a modest, hard-working, talented student. Like an antique collector hearing praise of one of his treasures, Lao Shen chuckled whenever anyone mentioned Fan's name.

"This is a new painting by Professor Pan," said Fan, pointing to a picture beside hers.

It was a landscape. But it looked more like a gaudy quilt hanging in a display case at a dry-goods shop: just a hodgepodge of clashing primary colors, with hardly any use of dark ink. The paint was piled on so thick in some places that it was beginning to peel like skin afflicted with eczema. There was no art about it—the composition was banal, the lines weak. I could not imagine how Pan could have made such a vulgar painting. He usually modeled himself on Shi Tao[3] and Jian Jiang.[4] His brushwork had always been intriguing, and he was accomplished in the use of ink.

"What made him paint garbage like this?" I blurted out.

"First he painted a pretty good one called *A Prosperous Family*, with a strong use of ink, and quite artistic. But the attack on Lao Shen scared him into dashing off this one and using it instead."

Before I could express my disgust, it occurred to me to ask, "Where's Lao Shen's painting?"

"Over there. I'll show it to you." As we walked she whispered, "Night before last I went to his house to talk him into withdrawing from the show, but he wouldn't hear of it. I just can't understand why he's doing this. He usually doesn't care whether his paintings are on exhibit. Do you think he's looking for a showdown with Zhao Xiong?"

"I can't figure him out either. He's just asking for trouble."

"Have you heard that Zhao is coming to inspect the paintings today? I'm certain no good will come of it. Zhao is sure to find something wrong with Lao Shen's painting. Anyway, there's nothing we can do—it's here now."

As we rounded a corner, Fan pointed straight ahead. "Look, that's it. It's a great painting."

She was right. Lao Shen's painting presented a bold, refreshing vista: on the right was a vast empty golden desert; on the left were broad emerald fields. Dividing the two starkly contrasting worlds was a dark and dense wide belt of trees that stood tall in the foreground and stretched endlessly into the distance. I sensed a hot wind blowing a reddish haze of sand from the desert toward the green world on the left, but the forest belt acted as a giant screen to cleanse and tame the wind before it reached the fields. Best of all, although there was not a soul to be seen, the painting inspired respect for the creative power of the workers who had wrought such a miracle. And then there were the painter's expressive power, talent, daring, and his passion for life, labor, and the people. As with all masterpieces, one stood before it reverently with one's heart pounding in unison with the artist's.

I noticed that I was surrounded by a crowd of people, all engrossed in the painting. With relief I concluded that no fault could be found with it, neither in content nor in artistic technique. Only a madman who hallucinated bombs dropping in the picture could denounce it.

A babble of voices awakened me from my reverie. The sparkling glass doors of the exhibition hall had been thrown open, and a crowd was pouring in. The people near the doorway stepped aside quickly, as if for a police car with a screeching siren. There were whispers of "Out of the way!"

"Secretary Zhao is here," Fan Ying murmured to me.

I know that readers dislike the use of caricature to describe a boor, since a candid display of the narrator's prejudices detracts from a character's believability and depth. Therefore I would like to assert that in this account I have done my best to avoid the techniques of caricature—such as disfigurement, exaggeration, and ridicule. I have simply recorded what I saw and felt that day. If my story seems to smack of caricature, that is because life itself was freakish in those days. Anyone who lived through those times can attest to the plausibility of what I am about to narrate. In that topsy-turvy cultural vacuum, life was full of far more preposterous happenings than this.

I spotted him coming in the doorway: a big, beefy,

red-faced, middle-aged man. He wore a black wool overcoat with a leather collar and a handsome otter-fur hat.
The green scarf around his neck was eye-catching, and
his shoes were shiny. But the overall effect was disgust-
ing. His expensive new clothes only enhanced his vul-
garity. His smug face was the picture of health, and he
had the exuberance that comes with success. I had heard
that he was in his late forties, but his skin was as smooth
as a new porcelain jar. He was surrounded by a crowd,
and he glanced about happily, greeting people and ac-
knowledging their respectful hellos, inquiries, and smiles.

An attendant presented him with a brocade album
and an ink-filled writing brush, and asked him to sign
in. He made a few dabs as if painting a lucky charm,
then returned the album and brush to the attendant.

"I'm here," he called out shrilly, raising one big hand,
"to learn from you, comrades!"

A short, thin, middle-aged man in glasses next to him
shouted, "Secretary Zhao has taken time from his busy
schedule to view the art show personally and to give us
his instructions. We extend our warmest welcome to
him!" He had a slight southern accent.

There was a round of applause. Some people even
forced admiring smiles, while others went forward to
shake hands with Secretary Zhao as if hoping some of
his glory would rub off on them. Then, guided by Director Yang and Vice-Director Ma of our institute and
some officials from the Municipal Cultural and Educa-
tional Section and Cultural Bureau, Zhao began to review the paintings. He walked with his hands behind

his back, confidently tossing off opinions as he went. The short thin man with him carried a little notebook, in which he scribbled rapidly, afraid of missing a word.

"Now this is a good painting! But the person looks a little weak—the arms are too thin. They don't look like working-class arms. And the face should be bigger, no more little noses and eyes—we must express the spirit of the age. The face needs more color too. Don't be afraid of red! Somebody said, 'The people in today's paintings look like Guan Gong.'[5] Was he right?" Zhao turned on Director Yang, as if the question were aimed at him. Director Yang smiled without answering; he knew that the secretary was so opinionated and capricious that it was difficult even to be his yesman. "That was a very reactionary thing to say!" continued Zhao with a frown. "A red age should have red people! Look like Guan Gong? That's malicious slander of the Revolution. Go home and check up on who made that remark."

The leaders of the art world around him had to nod in agreement, and the atmosphere grew tense. Some people began to sneak out of his way. Fan and I stayed where we were, but we could hear everything he said—his voice was loud and the crowd hushed. The paintings hung in silence awaiting his verdict.

They had already viewed half the paintings when they arrived at Fan's. This was a fateful moment for her. I glanced worriedly at her, but her pretty face was calm. Her long lashes were fluttering, but her gaze was as blank as if she were staring at a nondescript landscape.

"This is the work of a member of our junior faculty,"

I heard Director Yang explain. "She is committed to working from life and has made great progress recently. Most people think highly of this painting."

He was obviously trying to protect Fan.

Zhao nodded. Thank heaven, I thought, for once he didn't shake his head.

"Good!" he said. "We have to let go and give the young generals a chance. We have to admit that old people are no use anymore. There's nothing strange about it: the new supersedes the old. During the seventeen years of counterrevolutionary dictatorship,[6] some old artists were lauded to the skies. Now we can see that they weren't so great after all. What a hoax! All that blather about 'fine brushwork' and . . . and . . . 'marvelous ink' and 'inno—' what?—oh, yes, 'innovative composition.' And—all of it nonsense, a deaf chorus of praise. Why didn't their art seem great to me? We musn't let them lead us astray and suppress the young generation. With people like that blocking the way, how can the young people ever get ahead?"

He seemed to have forgotten to inspect Fan's work closely. His gaze fell on the next painting, that dreadful creation of Pan's.

"Bravo!" shouted Zhao. Everyone flinched. It sounded like the cheering of a chance audience watching a martial arts performance in the streets. "Really pretty! Pretty!" he repeated, beaming. "Now this is beautified art!" (Not my malapropism—those were his very words.) "A splendid landscape! Great, who painted this one?"

196

"Pan Danian," answered Director Yang. "Another member of the faculty of our Traditional Chinese Painting Department. He's right here." He turned and beckoned to Pan.

I now saw that Pan was in the crowd behind Zhao. He elbowed his way quickly over to Zhao and shook hands with him respectfully. "I'm Pan Danian," he said with a smile, "I would be grateful for your criticism, Secretary Zhao." He looked tense, and the smile was forced.

"Your painting is very good, different from all the traditional Chinese paintings I've ever seen. It captures the spirit of the times. Traditional Chinese painting is a product of feudalism, a bastion of conservatism—it's about time it was revolutionized. But I'm talking about proletarian revolution. Not bourgeois revolution—absolutely not. You must have been told what I said when I was inspecting the paintings at the new hotel. There was one by your colleague Shen Zhuoshi, a view of the Li River surrounded by big black mountains. I said it was no good, but some people defended him, saying he was using—what was that now?—oh, yes, 'backlighting.' Why would someone paint 'backlighting'? Does he have his back to the sun? What does that mean?[7] Besides, everybody knows the scenery along the Li River is green, so why did he make it black? The person defending him said this was 'creative.' He was just hawking capitalist goods in the name of reforming traditional, feudal Chinese painting. We must be on our guard! And some people say, 'Ink is paramount in traditional Chinese painting.' Who made that rule? That's one of the conventions set by the feudal classes—we proletarians must smash them! I think that the revolution in traditional Chinese painting has to start by limiting the use of ink.[8] I've heard that when the record of my comments on the paintings at the new hotel was transmitted at your institute, some people stubbornly refused to accept my point of view. I'm a firm believer in democracy: when I'm wrong, I hope people will let me know. Tell me please, how many of the things around us are black? Are there black flowers? Or leaves? Or mountains? Or rivers? Why would anyone paint them black? I think it's because the painter is blackhearted! Pan Danian, this painting of yours is a model. We need many more like it. This is the beginning of a thoroughgoing revolution in traditional Chinese painting!''

Pan stood there awkwardly, his features contorted in a shamefaced smile. He tried to speak but stammered and fell silent.

Zhao turned to Director Yang. "Is there anything by Shen Zhuoshi here?"

"Yes, over there." The group moved clumsily in a semicircle and stopped in front of Lao Shen's painting. Fan and I stood to one side watching anxiously. But I was certain that Lao Shen's painting was beyond reproach. Unless Secretary Zhao was superhuman.

Zhao stood sullenly, arms folded, left hand cupping his right elbow, right hand absentmindedly stroking his smooth fleshy chin. His eyes grimly scanned the painting, a searchlight looking for enemy planes in the night sky. "What kind of picture is this?" he demanded after a long silence. "There are no people in it. I can't understand it!"

I thought to myself, It's not that you can't understand it, it's that you can't find anything wrong with it.

Just as Director Yang stepped forward to explain the painting, Zhao turned and asked with a sneer, "Is Shen Zhuoshi here?"

"Where's Shen Zhuoshi? Is he here?" shouted Zhao's henchman.

An ominous sign.

Director Yang asked the people around him. Then someone said, "He's here." And we saw him. He had been there all along, standing alone at the other end of the hall. He looked frail despite his faded blue, padded overcoat. On the crown of his head was a brown Russian hat, his forehead bulging from under its brim. Around his neck was a long black scarf, one end of which hung down in front of his chest and the other was flung over his shoulder—just the way he had looked in our student days in the forties.

All eyes were upon him, all of them worried. Although Zhao was glowering at him, Lao Shen stood his ground for a moment before making his way slowly forward. He stopped about six or seven paces from Zhao. I was afraid he was going to say something that would offend Zhao.

"Did you paint this?" demanded Zhao.

"Yes," answered Lao Shen with a nod.

"What do you think of this painting of yours?"

"The evaluation of a work of art should be up to the viewer. It's not for me to say." Lao Shen's reply was camouflaged back talk. His audacity was shocking.

"All right," said Zhao irascibly, biting his lip. "I'm a viewer too. May I make a suggestion?"

"Of course. Please do," answered Lao Shen calmly.

Zhao pointed behind him at the painting. "Your painting contains a serious error!" he bellowed.

I winced and noticed Fan shudder beside me as if struck in the chest by an arrow.

"Error?" Lao Shen seemed startled. "What error?"

The left side of Zhao's mouth curled in a sneer. His eyes flashed with self-satisfaction. "Tell me this: what is the hallmark of the present world-revolutionary situation?"

"What do you mean by asking me that?" countered Lao Shen, frowing doubtfully. He looked uneasy.

"Oh, so you're going to play dumb! All right, let me put it this way: would you say that 'the east wind prevails over the west wind'[9] in the world today or that 'the west wind prevails over the east wind'?"

"Of course 'the east wind prevails over the west wind.'"

Despite his decisive answer, Lao Shen's furrowed brow did not relax. Fan's pretty face was also veiled in confusion. No one understood what Zhao was driving at.

"Then why did you paint a west wind?" Zhao finally asked.

"West wind? What west wind?" asked Lao Shen angrily, his voice rising.

"What? Getting scared? Did you think the message of your painting would escape me? Still want to deny it? Tell me, which way is the wind blowing the leaves in your painting? To the left! 'Left for a west wind, right for an east wind.' That makes this a west wind, doesn't it? So there!"

I had never heard such a preposterous, terrifying critique of a painting—but in those days this was the standard treatment of art and artists. It was done brazenly, in broad daylight, and before huge audiences. Overnight, the civilized world had become ten times more barbaric than the Middle Ages. Civilization, conscience, and reason almost died out. As for you, Art, what else would they demand of you?

Fan was blushing angrily, and her lashes were fluttering. She moved to step forward and defend Lao Shen. I reached over and grabbed her coattail to stop her.

"That would be suicide!" I whispered in her ear.

The remark seems ridiculous to me now. How could the discussion of a painting be a matter of life and death? But that was the way it was in those days. Before my very eyes, injustice, humiliation, and cruel persecution were rolling in an avalanche toward Lao Shen.

Lao Shen's surprise had turned into anger. I knew him well enough to realize that he would never stand for such slander. His mouth was twisted in an involuntary grimace, and his forehead was flushed. He was going to fight back. After a few searching glances at Zhao's crude shiny face, his eyes suddenly flashed as an idea struck him. The anger faded from his face, his composure returned, and a scornful dimple played on his cheek.

"Why don't you answer the secretary's question?" demanded Zhao's henchman, stepping forward. His tone was even harsher than Zhao's. "A dog is always fiercer that its master," says the adage.

"Answer what?" asked Lao Shen coolly.

"Are you trying to play stupid? The secretary asked you why you painted a west wind."

"I didn't, it's an east wind," answered Lao Shen with a deadpan face, putting his hands behind his back. What was he talking about? I was baffled along with everyone else.

"It's obviously a west wind. 'Left for west and right for east.' Don't try to weasel out of this!" roared Zhao.

Lao Shen smiled blandly. "In an east wind the trees bend toward the west," he said clearly and deliberately.

A hush fell over the hall as the crowd considered what he had said. Then people began to murmur. He was right! In an east wind the trees bent toward the west. Zhao had bluffed everyone into thinking that there was no room for argument. Heads nodded automatically in agreement with Lao Shen. But I knew that Lao Shen's "argument" had been forced out of him. He had made it up on the spur of the moment. I admired his presence of mind, yet I was troubled to see an artist pushed into such a corner.

Zhao was utterly defeated—by a truism, by an undeniable natural phenomenon. Lao Shen was an old boxer dodging before his opponent could strike. For Zhao, this was more intolerable than a returned blow. He had missed his shot, been knocked off balance, and publicly humiliated. His face darkened.

"Secretary Zhao, let's move on to the other paintings," said Director Yang hastily. "If you don't like Lao Shen's painting, we can take it down." Director Yang was a timid, overcautious man.

"It's not that Secretary Zhao doesn't like the painting, it's that the painting contains an error," said Zhao's henchman. "Secretary Zhao said at the beginning that there are no people in the painting. That's an enormous error."

Afraid to answer, Director Yang stood in silence.

"Back to the Party Committee office!" ordered Zhao huffily with a wave of his arm, as he turned and strode toward the door. The hem of his coat flounced angrily. His entourage followed him in awed silence; the only sound was the patter of footsteps as they disappeared out the door. Just a few people were left in the hall, and all eyes were still upon Lao Shen. He looked unruffled. Untying his scarf, he tossed one end over his shoulder and retied it, then walked calmly toward the door. Fan went over to him, and I followed.

"You were wonderful! Professor Shen, how did you ever come up with that answer? You really shut him up!" whispered Fan, her eyes filled with admiration.

"What kind of answer was that? How absurd! He

forced it out of me. Never in my life have I stooped to such nonsense. And to think it actually worked! Ridiculous! But you've got to give people like him a taste of their own medicine," Lao Shen said with a chuckle.

He still had some of that youthful naiveté left. He sauntered out, pleased with himself. But I had a hunch that the worst was yet to come.

Premonitions and dreams are distorted reflections of reality. Sometimes they come true. My hunch about Lao Shen was absolutely right. Within a few days he was the target of a vicious campaign. The reports of it were so frightening that I could stay home no longer. On the pretext of going to the clinic for medicine, I went to the institute to see for myself. The campus was blazoned with big-character posters that read: "SHEN ZHUOSHI IS A CAPITALIST, RESTORATIONIST, BLACKENED ROOT IN OUR INSTITUTE!" "THE FACTS OF THE CLASS STRUGGLE IN THE TRADITIONAL CHINESE PAINTING DEPARTMENT MUST BE BROUGHT TO LIGHT!" and "SHEN ZHUOSHI MUST ADMIT HIS GUILT!" Each character was a good square yard in size. Other signs read: "A LIST OF SHEN ZHUOSHI'S CRIMES," "A SELECTION OF SHEN ZHUOSHI'S REACTIONARY REMARKS," and "SHEN ZHUOSHI'S EIGHTEEN CRIMES." I could see at a glance that most of them repeated slanderous charges that had been brought against Lao Shen early in the Cultural Revolution and of which he had long since been cleared. But here they were again. I was appalled. I thought, too, that I sensed a change in people's attitude toward me: they either avoided me or were lukewarm.

The next day someone from my department arrived to tell me that despite my illness I had to go to the institute to participate in the campaign. I did not dare disobey. When I got there the next morning, the leader summoned me and told me that I would have to expose Lao Shen's "reactionary conduct," since I had gone to school with him and was the only teacher in the Print Department who was close to him. But how could I participate in the frame-up of a good man just to save my own skin? I decided that no matter how great the pressure on me—even if I were punished along with him—I would not betray my friend.

I assumed that Fan and Pan had probably made the same decision. In front of the office building were more signs: "FAN YING, WAKE UP!" "YOU'RE IN FOR TROUBLE IF YOU PROTECT SHEN ZHUOSHI!" and "PAN DANIAN, IT'S TIME YOU FELL IN LINE!"

The Traditional Chinese Painting Department was very tense. There were meetings all day every day and sometimes at night. We could hear them shouting slogans at their rallies. I was worried about Lao Shen, but I believed that he could take it. He had weathered as many gales as that plum tree. But this storm was the most ferocious yet. I knew that in Beijing they had opened an exhibition of counterrevolutionary art and that a number of artists had been attacked. Lao Shen's misfortune was not an isolated phenomenon, nor was it to be dismissed lightly. That was why I feared for his survival. The strongest will can be broken. Walking across campus I would take my time, hoping to run into Lao Shen or Fan or Pan and find out what was happening.

At the end of one workday, I ran into Pan as he was coming out of the east exit of the office building and I was coming out of the south exit. It looked as if our paths would cross at the campus gate. Delighted, I estimated the distance and paced myself so that we would meet. But when Pan saw me he stopped and, pretending not to have seen me, began to fumble in his pockets as if he had forgotten something. He hurried back into the building. I saw through his act. He was afraid contact with me might mean trouble for him. I began to suspect that he would harm Lao Shen. Of course it was just another hunch, but I had my reasons.

Although Pan and I were schoolmates, I had distrusted him for a long time. In the twenty years that we had known each other we had never argued. He always agreed with whatever I said, yet I was never as close to him as I was to Lao Shen, who was as pugnacious as a bulldog. There was always an invisible wall between Pan and me. We politely kept each other at arm's length, neither wanting to take a step closer. And I had something else against him because of a past incident. . . .

It happened early in the Cultural Revolution, when the three of us were locked up in the same "cow shed." One winter day there came an order to conserve coal. The student-warders told us to cut down on our use of hot water. But Lao Shen went ahead and mixed the cold tap water with the leftover boiled water from the thermos. After lunch he was summoned to an interrogation. While dozing on my plank bed, I was dimly aware that Pan was squatting in front of a stool writing a note, which he took out to the student-warder.

"Imagine reporting such trivia. Get back in there!"

This woke me up. I watched Pan come sullenly back into the room. Wondering what he had reported, I feigned sleep and listened carefully but heard nothing. After a while Pan was also escorted off for questioning. The student-warder happened to leave for a moment, and I found myself alone. I got up and went to the door for a look. The note was lying on a chair. I scanned it rapidly and was appalled by the message of the squared-off, little characters, written with a blunt pencil:

I hereby report that instead of conserving coal, Shen Zhuoshi gargled with hot water this morning. This is a grave offense.

Informant: Pan Danian

I was disgusted. I had not dreamed that pressure could turn a man into such a shameless wretch. For many days afterward I gave Pan the cold shoulder—which mystified Lao Shen. I did not want to tell him what I knew, but, since they were close friends and colleagues, I did drop a few hints.

"He's just a little timid. It's the flaw in his personality," Lao Shen said with a chuckle.

I tried to counter this without revealing my secret. "Yes, I agree with you, but that's not all there is to it. It's often a sign of selfishness. If such a person lacks firm convictions, he may very well betray a friend."

"Ha ha! Don't jump to conclusions. Everyone is selfish. Anyway, Danian's good points far outweigh his bad ones. Don't be too hard on him. At the beginning of the Cultural Revolution, Danian joined in the attacks against me. If you say he did it because he was timid and wanted to protect himself, I believe it—and I forgive him. The campaign was so ferocious, how many people could withstand it? Especially since he's rather weak. But I don't consider it a betrayal. You know, he has cried in front of me so many times—" Lao Shen's mouth was quivering. I had only succeeded in arousing his sympathy for Pan.

Oh, Lao Shen! I thought, but held my tongue. I figured that even if I did tell him, he would probably forgive Pan. In matters of the heart, Lao Shen was very stubborn. So I said no more, but my guard was up against Pan.

So Pan's deliberate avoidance of me now aroused real anxieties. In those days betrayal by one's close friends or relatives was a fatal blow. But as best as I could remember, Pan had no evidence to present against Lao Shen. Maybe he was avoiding me simply out of his usual timidity. Still, I had no way of finding out what was happening with Lao Shen. Apparently I would have to run into Lao Shen himself.

I finally bumped into him in the first-floor corridor

of the office building. We were walking toward each other. We were the only people around. It was a windy day and the corridor was drafty. Lao Shen was wearing his long black scarf, but he was bareheaded and his hair was windblown. I stopped and waited for him. When he reached me he paused briefly to look directly at me. His eyes were bloodshot, the obvious result of many sleepless nights. But his gaze was still bright and piercing. It radiated self-confidence, pride, and invincibility. I sensed that he was trying to encourage me. Then, grabbing the end of the scarf that hung down in front of his chest, he flung it over his shoulder and hurried away.

Two days later I bumped into him again. Again there was no one else around, and again he did not talk to me. I also saw Fan once, but she just frowned, bit her lip, and gave me a furtive nod. I was not sure what she meant, but guessed that all was not well with Lao Shen. I knew that Lao Shen and Fan were refraining from speaking to me to keep me from being implicated, while Pan was avoiding me to keep his nose clean.

After about a fortnight, the campaign seemed to be winding down. They were having fewer rallies at the Traditional Chinese Painting Department, and the signs around campus had been ripped to shreds by the cold wind. And then the commotion started all over again. Rumor had it that Lao Shen had committed a crime: making "counterrevolutionary paintings" with "highly reactionary" content. New signs and big-character posters appeared in the yard. One read: "THERE IS IRON-CLAD PROOF THAT SHEN ZHUOSHI PAINTS COUNTERREVO-

LUTIONARY PAINTINGS!" Did that ever look awesome in black and white! That night some amateur artists from nearby factories came to my house to ask about the campaign. News traveled fast because Lao Shen had many admirers.

But I was baffled. What counterrevolutionary paintings?

At about four o'clock the next afternoon, following a meeting, I was told to go to the little exhibition hall in the North Main Building to see the exhibition of counterrevolutionary paintings by Shen Zhuoshi. When I got there I found almost two hundred people waiting to go in—all of them grave and silent. The atmosphere was constrained and funereal.

The first thing we saw when we got inside was a sign that purported to "explain" Lao Shen's "crimes." There were forty or fifty paintings on exhibit, including his rough drafts and classroom sketches. They even had his drawings of nudes from twenty years before at art school. These were labeled "pornography." I wondered where they had dug them up—they had probably searched his house again. Beneath each painting was a square label pointing out its "crime." The accusations were totally unconvincing. One painting depicting twelve chicks running down a hill was said to "insinuate that the May Seventh policy was going downhill." I could not figure out what chicks had to do with the May Seventh policy until a colleague explained it to me: five plus seven equals twelve, and he had painted twelve chicks running downhill.[10] That was his crime. The label beneath the painting read: "This is the kind of under-handed method Shen Zhuoshi uses to attack new revolutionary developments." The sight sent cold shivers down my spine.

There were also the paintings that Lao Shen had made for the new hotel. I had never seen them before. They were superb. Their bold, powerful style experimented with the new while preserving the traditions of Chinese painting. They were so daring and successful that a crowd of students had gathered before them. I could tell by their eyes that they were enjoying the paintings and studying them surreptitiously instead of repudiating them. They obviously regarded this show as a rare learning opportunity. I even heard people softly clicking their tongues in admiration. I was proud of Lao Shen. He would have liked to have seen this.

One spot near the exit had attracted a particularly large crowd. I heard a couple of students whispering near me.

"Look, that's the 'counterrevolutionary painting.' I heard that he gave it to someone, and that person turned it in."

"Who? Who would do a mean thing like that?"

"I don't know, but it must have been someone close to him. He gave it to the person!"

"Someone close to him! A friend? Hm!" The second student snorted contemptuously.

Their conversation jogged my memory. Foreboding surged through me like an electric current. With a shudder I elbowed my way quickly through the crowd and looked. There hung *Plum Blossoms in the Snow*, Lao Shen's gift to Pan. The message of the painting was obvious at a glance. This was grounds for them to destroy Lao Shen.

I felt a stabbing pain in my heart and my vision blurred. I don't even remember how I left the exhibition. As I walked across campus I heard angry whispers about Pan. But who was whispering and what they were saying I can no longer remember; I don't think I heard clearly at the time.

Leaving the institute by the main gate, I wandered along the embankment outside. As night fell, a piercing north wind rose, but I ignored it. A painful question whirled around in my mind: Why? Could a friend of more than twenty years' standing let you down? Did you have to pay with your life before you could see some people for what they really were? And I hated myself: Why had I refrained from telling Lao Shen my opinion of Pan? And why had I not heeded my sense of foreboding and stopped Lao Shen from giving the painting to Pan? Wasn't I also to blame for this? I too had harmed Lao Shen.

I did not return from the river until after dark. I stopped at a dumpling shop along the way, but instead of dumplings I ordered a drink and a plate of pickles. I never frequented taverns, but that night I wanted to get drunk. After a couple of drinks I noticed the conversation of two workers at my table, burly middle-aged men in coarse grimy workclothes, who held their little glasses to their lips in big dirty hands. Their scarlet faces said that they had already had a good deal to drink. They were deriving great satisfaction from cursing some traitor. I felt as if they were speaking for me too, and their talk did me more good than the alcohol.

"Excuse me," I said to them, my tongue loosened now, "what should I do if I run up against someone like the guy you're talking about?"

One of them—who had a broad face, heavy brows, and a dense growth of stubble—turned his bloodshot eyes to me. "People like that are wolves in sheep's clothing," he blustered. I could smell the liquor on his breath. "They're trash. You should go find him, grab him by the collar, give him one helluva good piece of your mind, and then beat him up!"

His vehement answer made my cheeks burn. With newfound energy I slapped the table, stood up, drained my flask of liquor, and strode out of the restaurant to look for Pan.

When I got to his house I banged on the door as hard as I could. The sound was earsplitting.

An ashen face appeared at the door—it was Pan. He took a good look at me, and his features registered shock.

"What's the matter, Lao He? What's happened? Are you drunk? What made you do that? Come on in!"

Without answering, I grabbed him by the lapel and dragged him outside. I don't know where I got the strength. It was as easy as dragging an empty cardboard carton.

"Look what you've done, Pan!" I said, my voice shaking violently. "Tell me why you hurt Lao Shen! Why, why the hell did you do it?"

Pan shakily recovered his balance. He had never seen me so angry. He was scared, and for the first time I noticed how despicable his fat pale face was and how treacherous those small eyes of his were.

"Lao He," he pleaded, trying to look pathetic and remorseful, "calm down and listen to me. I—uh—didn't have any choice. The pressure was too much for me."

His plea made me even angrier. The liquor rushed to my head.

"You bastard!" I bellowed. But I could not say any of the things I had planned to say. My lips, my tightly clenched fists—my whole body was trembling violently.

"Lao He, please put yourself in my shoes for a minute. I—I'm a family man!"

I spat into his face. Then I turned quickly and stalked away. He followed me, begging.

"Lao He, wait a minute, please—"

"Get lost!" I roared at him. "Next time, why not betray me too!"

I strode stiffly away, stumbling as I went. Liquor and anger were boiling in my veins. I was still trembling, and tears were streaming from my eyes. I did not know why I was crying, but I let the tears roll without wiping them away. As I walked I began to despise myself for lacking the courage of the two workers I had just met. Why hadn't I used my fists and given him the thrashing of his life?

On a cold snowy day the next winter, I went to visit Lao Shen for the first time in a year.

I had another attack of angina when I got home from Pan's house that night. I felt as if a knife were being twisted in my chest; the pain was worse than it had ever been before. If my wife had not gotten me my nitroglycerin in time, I probably would not have survived the night. For a while I was so ill that I could not endure the least upset, not even loud voices. One of my sons, who is a farmer in my hometown near Mount Wuyi in Fujian, came and took me back with him. He nursed me for a full year.

The school sent two people to Fujian to ask me about the circumstances surrounding the composition of Lao Shen's *Plum Blossoms in the Snow*. I said, "Everyone knows that plum blossoms are hardy. Bitter cold doesn't faze them. Lao Shen must have meant them to stand for the integrity of a revolutionary." That was all I would say. Fortunately they were both decent people. They hinted at a certain sympathy for Lao Shen and left without questioning me further. But they did not tell me what had happened to him.

That episode worried me. From my remote retreat in the blue-hazed hills I constantly thought of my endangered friend. I missed him as I watched the morning mist rising from the valleys or heard the evening crows cawing on their return to the forest; or when spring rain pattered on the roof; or when the frostbitten red autumn leaves floated into the window. I missed him most once after a big blizzard—when I found lovely, wild plum trees blooming in a silent white mountain pass. The red flowers perfumed the clear, cold air. I tried to imagine the terrible fate that had befallen him. Then I prayed to the flowers for his safety. The hardy plum blossoms were my only consolation.

The attack on Lao Shen, combined with the latest campaign to "counterattack the right-deviationist trend to reverse correct verdicts,"[11] made those days extraordinarily oppressive. Society was in such upheaval that there was no telling what might happen next. My family urged me to give up art, calling it too dangerous. My son accompanied me back to school to arrange for my retirement on grounds of illness. I would withdraw from the world of painting, move back to my old home, and become a hermit in these faraway hills with their fresh air, where I would just "enjoy the wind and the moon," as the saying goes.

The tension and gloom at school were worse now than a year before. The heads of the school had all been intimidated by the latest campaign, and no one was willing to make a decision about my retirement. It looked as if I would not be able to make all the necessary arrangements in one visit. So I decided to go back to Fujian, taking my wife with me to avoid trouble.

I made some discreet inquiries about Lao Shen.

I found out that he had been sequestered since the day of the exhibition of counterrevolutionary paintings. Innumerable rallies had been held to make him confess to his crimes, but he had refused. Because of this, the story went, Secretary Zhao had been furious with the heads of our institute, particularly with Director Yang. Zhao suspected that Yang was protecting Lao Shen. Everyone knew that Director Yang respected the old professors in our school and that he was reluctant to treat Lao Shen too harshly. But neither did he dare stand up for him, in public or in private.

Then Zhao attended a rally at our school. After that, black X's covered Lao Shen's name on all the big-character posters. A fortnight later Lao Shen was declared an "active counterrevolutionary," stripped of all his duties, and sent to the maintenance and food service to do supervised hard labor. His daily work included hauling coal, emptying garbage, sweeping the campus, and cleaning the toilets. Fan was charged with protecting Lao Shen and sent to work as a cashier in the cafeteria. Pan kept his post on the faculty of the Traditional Chinese Painting Department. But he was notorious among the teachers and students. Everyone shunned him. His students even talked back sarcastically in class. He grew depressed and walked with his head bowed, as if to avoid meeting anyone's gaze. He seemed miserable.

It was all distressing news. I decided that before returning to Fujian I would visit Lao Shen no matter what. I knew he must be very much in need of a friend.

Dusting the snow from my cap and shoulders, I knocked on Lao Shen's door.

Mrs. Shen opened it. But she did not behave the way I

had expected her to—after all, one should show some excitement after a year of separation. She looked careworn, unfriendly, and listless.

"Is Lao Shen home?" I asked.

"He—" Mrs. Shen hesitated. I guessed that she did not want to let me see him.

Just then Lao Shen called out from inside, "Come in! Is that Lao He?"

"Yes, it's me, Lao Shen!" I cried.

Lao Shen ran out and grabbed me by the arm. "Come on in, Lao He!" he shouted excitedly, clasping hands with me.

"Can't you lower your voice?" Mrs. Shen said nervously. "Aren't you afraid someone will hear you?"

I understood. I motioned to Lao Shen that we should continue our conversation inside. He made a pot of tea. When we sat down together, we took a good look at each other. I suddenly felt sad: he had lost weight, and his black satin padded jacket, once tight, was now baggy. He had aged a great deal in a short time. His thin face was sunken and pasty, his cheekbones protruded even more than before. There were dark circles under his bloodshot eyes. His hairline had crept back farther, and what hair remained was even more disheveled and gray than before. I looked around. Mrs. Shen had also aged a great deal. The room was dimly lit, the fire in the stove had burned low, and there was a chill. The walls were bare: not a painting left, only nail holes where they had been. The draftsman's table by the wall was covered with newspaper and piled with a few dozen Chinese cabbages. Tears welled up in my eyes.

"What's wrong? You've been storing up that useless liquid too?"

Lao Shen's eyes flashed. I stopped crying right away. How I loved that sparkle in his eyes! Ashamed, I wiped away my tears with the back of my hand. He solicitously inquired about my illness and life in my hometown but did not speak of himself.

"What about you? You've said nothing about yourself. Are you pretending I don't know that you've been—"

"Cleaning toilets?" he interrupted quickly, then asked with a smile, "Do you think they can kill me that easily? What a foolish daydream. Ridiculous!" He laughed easily.

"But—" I glanced at the drab surroundings.

Lao Shen read my mind and chuckled mysteriously. "Oh, so you think—" And he looked as if he were about to give away a secret.

"All right," interrupted Mrs. Shen, "it's time to refill your hot-water bottle. You'd better change the water. Aren't you afraid you'll get a stomachache? You've only been better for a few days, and you're getting careless already."

Lao Shen stood up, took the green rubber hot-water bottle out of his jacket, and refilled it.

"Feeling no better than before?" I deliberately changed the subject.

Mrs. Shen answered for him. "Stomachache, high blood pressure, and a big mouth—the same three problems he's always had. Not one of them is better. Sooner or later they'll be the death of him."

"Enough," said Lao Shen, motioning to her impatiently to be quiet. "Why don't you stop talking and go get some wine? Lao He came a long way to see us, and he won't be here for long. You're being a terrible hostess."

I knew what was going on between them. I quickly made the excuse that the doctor had forbidden me to drink on account of my heart and told them not to go to any trouble. Mrs. Shen did not want to fetch the wine anyway. It was apparent that she was afraid to relinquish her watch over us. But Lao Shen insisted that she go. Finally she took a flask and huffily headed for the door.

"If things aren't bad enough for you already, then say whatever you want," she grumbled as she paused in the doorway. "Haven't you suffered enough on account of that painting and Pan Danian?" She left, slamming the door behind her.

I was embarrassed. Lao Shen said apologetically, "My wife is unhappy. Please don't mind her. She's been through a lot on my account. It's a good thing we don't have any children, because they would have had to suffer too—" His voice trailed off. He hung his head and fiddled with the ashtray on the table. Along with his head of disheveled salt-and-pepper hair, I was getting a glimpse of his depressed side.

"Pan did this to you!" I blurted out.

"No." He shook his head. "He did and he didn't."

"What? Isn't all this because he sold you out?"

"He sold me out, but he sold himself out too."

"But he's fine, and you've suffered terribly!"

Lao Shen forced a smile. "Do you think he's happy? No, selling your soul is a dismal business. I bump into him all the time. He never so much as dares to look at me. If I stare at him deliberately, it scares him so that he skulks away with his tail between his legs. I'm the one who's got the upper hand. I can hold my head high. Isn't that strange? Here *I'm* the 'target of the dictatorship'! Do you think that this is a case of 'spiritual victory,'[12] like A Q's? No, of course it isn't. It proves that I should still be self-confident. As for your comment—am I 'suffering'? In one sense I've suffered plenty. But what no one will ever know is that I'm still happy—"

"Happy?" I asked, baffled. Maybe he really was fooling himself with the notion of 'spiritual victory.' What did he have to be happy about? I looked up at him doubtfully. His eyes were bright. Before I could ask him what he meant, he jumped up and took me by the hand.

"Come into the bedroom," he said excitedly.

Opening the curtain in the bedroom doorway, he led me inside and switched on the light. The room was small, about eight square yards. I stood in the narrow space between the bed and the wall and looked around: the bed was piled with quilts, and there was an old round alarm clock on the night table. One wall was covered with a coarse gray woolen blanket that hung on metal rings from a heavy wire. I assumed it was for insulation from the cold. There was nothing else in the room.

"What are you doing?" I asked.

Lao Shen smiled mysteriously, then bent over and opened the bedside table. It was crammed with art supplies: a brush holder, a water basin, an ink stone, and paint dishes. The basin was full of water, the paint dishes had lovely fresh paint in them, and black ink glistened on the ink stone. But what was he using them for?

I looked at him inquiringly.

He motioned for me to stand by the bed. Then he pulled the big gray blanket aside with a swish. I felt my eyes light up as a vast April landscape appeared before me. The dingy little room was gone, and the walls seemed to move rapidly outward and disappear. I felt bathed in the balmy spring sunshine that shone on the mountains and fields. I stood lost in this magnificent universe, and it was some time before I remembered that I was looking at a gigantic, lifelike painted scene. My response excited Lao Shen. Taking off his shoes, he climbed up on the bed and lifted up the painting to reveal yet another equally dazzling one underneath. He showed me one after another. Each one was almost three yards square. I can hardly describe what I felt as I looked at these paintings. I could smell the forest air and the delicate fragrance of endless fields of wheat and the bewitching perfume of clusters of flowers. I could hear the twittering of hundreds of birds, the thundering of waterfalls, the mighty roar of the sea, and the buzz of electricity in wires crisscrossing the plains. I was overwhelmed.

Lao Shen was lifting the huge paintings one by one and chattering away with boyish pride.

"Look over here—I got the idea of inlaying primary colors from handicrafts. And look at this: I used such a thick coat of burnt ink that it reflects. Do you think it's all right? This was a technique used by Gong Banqian.[13] Don't just stand there, tell me what you think of them!"

I looked up at him. He was standing on the bed, his face next to the light bulb that hung down from the ceiling. His cheeks were flushed and his eyes were glittering. He had totally forgotten that he was under surveillance. Even his present predicament had not stopped him in his quest for innovation.

"How did you paint such huge paintings?" I asked, my voice trembling.

He let go of the paintings. "I painted them on the wall, otherwise there wouldn't have been enough room. For the places I couldn't reach, here's what I did—" Standing on tiptoe on the edge of the bed, he reached up and moved his wrists, going through the motions of painting. Then he jumped down off the bed. "I did all these just in the last month," he told me as he put on his shoes. "I've painted forty or fifty over the past year. Look—" He lifted the sheet that hung over the edge of the bed. I bent down and peered inside: there were four huge rolls of paintings, each as thick as a telephone pole. He had wrapped them in plastic tied with cloth strips or rope to keep them dry.

As I looked, he reminded me of a member of the Red underground in the days before 1949. This room resembled an underground printing press, where he worked passionately, ignoring the danger all around him. He did manual labor in the daytime, so he must have made the paintings late at night. I looked again at his bloodshot eyes; the paintings were the fruit of his refusal to waste his imagination on dreams. The wire along the top of the wall had been polished shiny by the rings on the wall-blanket. It had obviously been pulled back and forth thousands of times.

Then Lao Shen pointed behind me. There hung a very familiar square painting: *Plum Blossoms in the Snow*. He had hung it there while I'd had my back turned.

"I painted a second one," he explained before I could open my mouth.

This one was even better than the first. The blizzard was wilder, the plum tree hardier, and the flowers more splendid. He had answered all my questions again with this painting. This time it seemed to have even more to tell me. I looked at him admiringly, but he avoided my gaze.

"Lao He," he said humbly, "don't imagine I'm some kind of superman. After Pan sold me out, my house was searched once more, and I was driven out of the department again. For a while I was very depressed, but

I got better. I came back with more energy than before. But I didn't recover all on my own. The people gave me friendship and strength, guided me and encouraged me. Don't you see?"

I shook my head. He was all alone. The notion of "the people" was far too abstract for me.

He led me outside into a narrow passageway. Snow was still whirling in the air, and a thick crunchy layer of it blanketed the ground.

We arrived at his backyard, which was less than four yards square. We stood in the center, enveloped in whiteness. I was about to ask why he had brought me out into the cold when I noticed little points of red in the twilight. As I looked, they grew clearer and brighter: plum blossoms! I realized that I was surrounded by little plum trees, some in pots, others in wooden crates. Two, which were as tall as a man, had been planted in the ground. The sturdy trunks and branches, which looked as if they were drawn in ink, were unbowed despite the weight of the snow. The flowers were in full bloom; the driving blizzard only enhanced their beauty. The cold damp air was perfumed with a fragrance that lingered despite the wind, as though it were too heavy to be blown away.

"Look, all these plum trees were gifts from people. They started to bring them to me secretly right after that exhibition of counterrevolutionary paintings. These two planted ones I got a year ago—they've been blooming especially well this winter. Sometimes when I'm tired after working late, I come out here at night and stand among the plum blossoms. I get my second wind. Just think, why did people give me these even though my *Plum Blossoms in the Snow* was denounced? Was it just because they liked my painting? No, you figure the answer out for yourself! Now you see why I said I was happy a little while ago."

That stormy night I bade Lao Shen a tearful farewell. I asked him for a sprig of plum blossoms, which I took back home and put into a gourd-shaped Longquan vase. The flowers bloomed for a long time before they finally wilted. Soon afterward I heard the news that Lao Shen was dead. In my grief I imagined that the wilting of the plum blossoms had been an omen of his death. But actually, Lao Shen died in the aftermath of a great historical event. He drank himself to death for sheer joy when he heard that the Gang of Four had fallen.

The news seemed terribly sudden, and terribly brief, because it came to me in a letter from a colleague, who provided none of the details. And by that time Lao Shen had been dead for more than a month. It was too late for a telegram of condolence, so I wired $100 to Mrs. Shen, but the money was returned as "undeliverable at this address." Worried, I dashed off a letter to Fan Ying, who answered promptly, saying that Mrs. Shen had gone to Beijing to stay with a nephew. She also filled in some of the details of Lao Shen's death. When he heard that the Gang of Four had fallen, he sat up all night drinking and laughing, despite Mrs. Shen's pleas. Finally he passed out and never woke up again. Fan, who saw him right after his death, said he looked "peaceful, as though he were asleep, with a smile on his face, but also somewhat bitter." Her description enabled me to picture him as if I had seen him with my own eyes.

Of course these were all events of the past.

For two years I received considerate letters from school, welcoming me to rejoin the faculty when my health is better. How could I resist the urge to snatch up my brush and use my few remaining years to create some beauty for our country? One day I packed my bags to go back to school and told my son to buy train tickets for that afternoon.

"What's the hurry?" he asked.

"I have to get there in time to see your Uncle Shen's painting show. I can't see him anymore, but I don't want to miss his show."

"But you've seen all of his paintings already."

"You don't understand. I—" I felt that nothing I could say would make a child understand all that Lao Shen and I had been through together. "Don't talk back," I said impatiently. "I just want tickets for today. If there are no seats I'll stand!"

I was standing before *Plum Blossoms in the Snow* again.

"Lao Shen," I addressed him silently, "do you know what is happening in our country today? If only you were still alive. How would you feel if you were?"

The painting was silent. But in the picture the blizzard seemed to stop, and the icy peaks began to thaw. The painting was giving off a brilliant light, filling the room with color. I refocused my eyes. The combined effect of all the paintings in the room had dazzled me momentarily. I looked at the painting again: the sturdy branches were trembling and the flowers sparkling like smiling eyes. . . .

Plum Blossoms in the Snow had silently answered me for the third time.

Nectar

I never used to touch a drop of alcohol, so I had no idea why people liked to drink such fiery stuff. I had watched many a red-faced, blustering drunk stagger around a restaurant, unable to stand even with help from his friends. Still worse were the foulmouthed sots who swore and carried on and made total fools of themselves. I figured that booze must be dreadful if a shot of "cat piss" could turn a dignified, self-respecting man into such a disgraceful wreck. The ancients dubbed it "nectar," but I decided that whoever came up with that one must have been sloshed himself. A teetotaler always won my instant approval, while a braggart who prided himself on how much he could guzzle got only a disdainful sneer from me.

In 1966 the Red Guards closed the taverns and banned drinking. The winos had to keep their gripes to themselves. I heard that some of them were stealing rubbing alcohol from the hospitals. I didn't care for the Red Guards at all, but I did like prohibition.

Somebody once told me that liquor releases inhibitions and makes people violent. Although I couldn't really know exactly what he meant, his remark confirmed my hatred of drink. But . . . nothing in this world is immutable. People do change their minds, especially where prejudices are concerned. And there came a day when the magic brew induced me to have a change of heart.

One Sunday a colleague dragged me along to his old boss's house for a visit. On the way he told me that the boss was a very nice man who had suffered terribly during the last ten years[1] but had now been given a higher position than before. My colleague insisted that his visit was prompted by nostalgia rather than any desire to flatter his superiors.

The mere thought of such social calls is enough to make my hair stand on end. I'm a real stay-at-home, lacking in the social graces. I knew I would feel terribly uneasy in the home of a high official.

"No, thanks. I don't even know the man. You go ahead without me."

As we were walking along, with me repeating this for the third time, he grabbed me by the wrist and pressed the electric doorbell of an attractive little house.

The door opened. An unsmiling servant inquired who we were and why we had come. After inspecting our IDs, he said he would ask whether his boss wanted to see us. Then he went back inside, slamming the door in our faces. Just the sight of the freshly painted green door was already making me very uneasy. I wanted to turn and run. My colleague, however, took everything in stride, as though he were waiting in line at a theater to see an interesting show.

The door opened again and we were ushered in. Passing through a walled garden and a quiet hallway, we arrived at a modest living room. There I met my colleague's distinguished old boss: a bald, fat, ungainly old man who nonetheless looked imposing. He shook hands with us cordially.

"Sit down." He gestured toward the sofa.

I felt tense and inhibited. I had never felt this way in front of my own superiors. The only time I had ever felt anything similar was once when I had to talk to an administrator who came to inspect our factory. But even then I had been nowhere near as jittery as I was now. The higher the official, the more nervous I felt—was that it? How peculiar!

As soon as I was seated face-to-face with the man my body froze. I perched gingerly on the edge of my chair. My neck was as stiff as deadwood, and my arms lay paralyzed on my lap. I maintained this position for some time. I began to ache all over. My throat was parched. I tried to imagine the taste of something sour but found to my dismay that my salivary glands had dried up. The servant brought me a cup of tea. While my colleague and his old boss were absorbed in conversation I furtively snatched up the cup and drained it in a single gulp. Instead of quenching my thirst, however, it scalded my tongue and burned my esophagus.

The boss turned and slowly pointed a fat, stubby, creased finger at me.

"Where do you work?"

This direct question flustered me even more. I could hardly remember what I did for a living, and I seemed to have lost my voice. Fortunately my colleague answered for me.

"He works at the same place I do—he's a technician at our factory. His name is Feng. He's been wanting to meet you for a long time."

The boss nodded and smiled faintly, as if in polite welcome. His smile was a rare favor bestowed across a vast social gap. I forced a smile in return but sensed that my expression was not appealing: I could not control a nervous tic around the eyes. I was afraid the boss would find it objectionable.

I could think of nothing but getting the visit over with and being able to stretch my legs outside. Such prolonged tension was definitely harmful to my health. But my colleague was chattering away about everything that had happened to him since he had left his old boss. The mention of recent hardships led him to reminisce about the good old days. Naturally he also mentioned his old colleagues, scattered now like a flock of birds; since there was a story to tell about each, there was no end to the conversation. My colleague did most of the talking, but the boss was fascinated. Since he had been "in seclusion"[2] for so many years, he was curious about everything. I guess it goes without saying that when you're with your superiors, you'd best keep to subjects they're

interested in. Every name that the boss could produce
from the recesses of his mind elicited a newsy report
from my colleague. He reminded me of a wheel that
just keeps on spinning once you give it a gentle push.

I was totally uninterested in their conversation and
had nothing to contribute. I wanted to take my leave,
but I lacked the nerve to interrupt a conversation that
the old boss was enjoying. I was stuck there, like a
prisoner.

I glanced at the clock on the wall: ten minutes to
eleven. If I stayed until lunchtime I would have to sit
there for at least an hour. How could I possibly stand
it? And yet what could I do? While they were engrossed in their conversation I furtively moved my arms
and legs and shifted my weight. I felt somewhat better,
except that my left thigh was all pins and needles where
my arm had been pressing on it.

I hated myself: I was too shy and punctilious, perhaps even servile. These were self-perpetuating weak-
nesses. I decided to play my only trump card: patience.

I waited patiently.

Patience is a most uncomfortable virtue, but I resort
to it habitually. They say that it comes naturally to
weaklings, but I don't mind, since I've seen many a
strong man have recourse to it as well.

Soon another guest arrived, a tall vigorous man with
dark skin and bright eyes. He had kept his youthful
figure into middle age and looked fit and trim in his
clean well-pressed Mao suit. His black leather shoes

were as glossy as lacquer; he must have shined them carefully on his way out the door that morning. He seemed to be very familiar with the boss. As soon as he came in he cracked a joke with the servant, then dashed into the other room to play with a child whom I never saw, probably the boss's granddaughter.

I could tell, however, that he was the boss's subordinate rather than his friend. No matter how familiar people of different social stations are, you can always sense the distinction. Superiors are easier to tell apart from their inferiors than adults from children.

The boss's conversation with the newcomer bore out my hunch. I discovered that the newcomer's name was Liu and that he was a bureau chief in the boss's office— because the boss alternated between calling him "Bureau Chief Liu" and just "Liu." He looked uneasy when the boss addressed him as "Bureau Chief Liu," but he would cheer up when the boss called him simply "Liu." This proved that the boss was his superior, because "Bureau Chief Liu" would have been the preferred form of address from an inferior.

They kept to shoptalk. Liu was a decent sort, not at all obsequious. But everything he said was news to the boss. He seemed extremely resourceful and knowledgeable. He spiked his conversation with his own insights and suggestions. Whenever something he mentioned brought a frown to the boss's face, he would change the subject to cheer him up again. I had never seen such a go-getter. He didn't look shrewd for nothing.

They were oblivious to me and my colleague, which

gave us an opportunity to rise and take our leave. But my colleague had no intention of doing so; he seemed used to being ignored by his betters. I managed to make eye contact with him. But he just smiled and shook his head as though absorbed in a performance. He was listening to Liu's conversation more intently than the boss was. He unconsciously mimicked the boss's every nod, smile, and shake of the head, like a student learning a repertoire of facial expressions from an old actor.

Exasperated, I decided to ignore my colleague and boldly put an apologetic smile on my face. But just as I was about to stand up and say good-bye, the servant came in and announced that lunch was ready. This was our cue to leave, I figured. But to my surprise the boss invited us to stay. How could I presume to eat at a stranger's house, and how could I share a table with such a high official? I said I was expecting company at home.

"Eat here. Please stay, everybody," the boss said gravely. He seemed sincere. I could no more refuse him than a child could disobey an adult. Besides, my colleague was tugging on the back of my jacket to tell me to accept. I detected an excited gleam in his and Liu's eyes. Apparently to dine here was as glorious as partaking in a state banquet.

Submissively I followed them into a small room used exclusively for dining.[3] Heavy purple velvet curtains were looped back on a pair of shiny metal hooks. Gentle light filtered through a fine gauze inner curtain. The round dinner table was covered with a snow-white tablecloth. Along the wall was a set of armchairs for resting before and after meals. On the end tables were cigarette cases, ashtrays, and toothpick holders.

For me—a nobody whose entire family had to squeeze into a single room—dining in such magnificent surroundings raised my tension level to a new peak. To make matters worse, I was seated between my colleague and his boss. On the boss's side my body was as stiff as a rusty door, while on my colleague's side I was still alive and functioning. The sensation was extraordinary.

The servant brought me chopsticks and a small plate, and meat, vegetables, rice, and soup soon arrived.

"Help yourself.[4] Make yourself at home, just the way you do at my house," said my colleague.

I sensed that this remark was intended for the boss's ears rather than mine. I was afraid to reach for the food, as if I thought it might hurt me.

"Have some," said the boss, who was sitting on my left.

Another command! Had he been smiling, he would have seemed less peremptory. But his face was stony.

Obediently I took some stir-fried bean sprouts, mixed them with my rice, and slowly began to eat. I had taken so few that I soon finished and began to pick at the rice at the bottom of my bowl. Both Liu and my colleague ignored me completely. They were vying for the boss's attention and taking turns replenishing his bowl.

The boss was pleased. He grew more amiable, and some of the tension went out of the air. Feeling slightly more relaxed, I began to help myself to the food. Then the boss asked the servant to bring a bottle of liquor and a few more dishes. The liquor was brought right away.

"I'll bet you've never tasted this before," chortled the boss, bottle in hand. "It's called 'Drunken Liu Ling.'⁵ Ha! You all know who Liu Ling was, don't you? He was a heavy drinker, but this stuff would have been more than he could handle. This is my favorite drink. *Xifeng, gujing,* and *maotai*⁶ are nothing compared with this."

"In a package like that it must be good," said my colleague.

He was flattering the boss, but the packaging really was lovely. The spirits were crystalline, the bottle clear glass. On the belly of the long-necked bottle was an oval orange label with gold flowers and lettering, and a round white insert, like a full moon, depicting Liu Ling and a high-minded friend drinking while seated at a stone table in a forest. Despite the small size of the picture every detail was visible, right down to the beards and eyebrows. The bottle was wrapped in shiny cellophane. The packaging made the liquor seem rare and costly. Had the bottle contained fruit juice, I would have been ten times more pleased. Unfortunately its contents were anathema to me. But strange to say, at that moment my aversion was less violent than usual.

The servant uncorked the bottle and filled everyone's glass.

"I don't drink," I protested hastily.

Everyone started to pressure me, as people always did at banquets.

"No, I never touch the stuff. I'm a teetotaler."

In any other circumstances I would have launched into a tirade against drinking, but I felt too inhibited there. Even so, I had no intention of breaking my taboo.

"Try a little. It won't hurt you," the boss said with a chuckle.

He meant well. Why is the benevolence of your superiors more compelling than their command? Why does the concern of a big shot seem more valuable than that of an ordinary person? I felt tipsy without having touched a drop. Obediently I took a sip.

How did my first drink taste? It certainly had a bite to it! Like a ball of fire, it burned my mouth and I wanted to spit it out. But I swallowed it instead and felt it sear my throat, my esophagus, and then my stomach. My entire chest cavity felt burned out, as though I had swallowed a big mouthful of sulfuric acid. In terror I opened my mouth and gasped for breath.

"Take a big bite of food and you'll be all right," someone advised.

I was beyond caring who the speaker was.

I wolfed down some rice and helped myself to a huge piece of meat, which I stuffed into my mouth. Yet no one thought me rude—instead they all burst out laughing. Even the boss joined in. Their mirth was good-natured: they were having fun. With some relief I began to unwind.

I had never realized before how exhilarating alcohol could be. Liquor shimmered in the glass; its bouquet

perfumed the air; glasses clinked; and the gathering grew
more convivial. Faces flushed; eyes sparkled; tongues
were loosened and voices grew louder. Everyone was
talking out of turn and even interrupting the boss. The
boss seemed less remote and imperious. The food on the
serving platters was a mishmash from everyone's dis-
orderly chopsticks.

They initiated me into the pleasures of drink. Only
that first mouthful was hard to swallow; after that I
had no trouble and began to guzzle it down, not realizing how strong it was. Before long my cheeks were
burning, as if toasted over a hot stove.

"All right!" exclaimed my colleague, rising and picking up the bottle. "You're no teetotaler. You could drink
us all under the table. Come on, have some more."

He was shouting. He bore no resemblance to the man
who had been so deferential to the boss just a little while
before. He tried to refill my glass, but I covered it with
my hand to stop him. Then Liu, who was across from
me, reached over and pushed my hand out of the way.

"The strong bear the heaviest burden!" he cried. My
glass was filled to overflowing.

My cheeks were on fire. I didn't dare drink any more.

"Come on, my dear boy," said the boss, clapping a
warm gentle hand on my shoulder, "let's drink a toast.
But remember, bottoms up."

Such a high official calling me "my dear boy"? I was
overwhelmed. Impetuously I raised my glass, tilted my
head back, and tossed the liquor down my throat. It
no longer stung. By now it was a warm fragrant mixture

of pleasure and passion, a nectar of the gods. No sooner had it bombarded my stomach than it rose straight to my head, which began to buzz like a beehive. I reached for another bite of meat for a chaser but could no longer control my chopsticks. Like live worms, the slippery slices of meat kept squirming out of reach. Glancing up, I saw that the faces of all present, including the boss, looked like curious large red orbs. They were laughing, but I couldn't hear them. Were they talking? Their voices sounded muffled, as if heard through a wall. I fuzzily realized I was drunk. So this was how it felt: free and uninhibited, like being tossed about at sea or soaring through the air. My feet seemed to have left the ground, and my legs no longer seemed attached to me. I kicked the table and found that there was no feeling in my foot.

"Why is the table shaking?" The voice sounded like Liu's.

"You must have had too much to drink. How could the table be shaking?" giggled my colleague. His face was as red as a ripe tomato.

Liu pointed his chopsticks at me. "He's the one who's had too much to drink. Look, everybody, there's Guan Gong![7] He looks just like him." His speech was slurred, as though his tongue were the wrong size for his mouth. His scarlet face was swaying from side to side, but I realized that it might equally have been I who was doing the swaying.

I was about to answer when I felt a heavy hand on my left shoulder—the boss. Leaning on me, he lurched to his feet as though he had been hit by a bullet. In the stylized intonation of Beijing opera he declaimed loudly:

> *Guan Gong—his name is Guan Yu;*
> *His surname is Guan, his first name Yu, and he styles*
>   *himself Yunchang—*

Then he began a hoarse rendition of Qiao Guolao's aria from the Beijing opera *Sweet Dew Temple*:

> *He has a younger brother, the Marquis of*
>   *Hanshou;*
> *Whose Black Dragon Sword fills the gods with*
>   *woe. . . .*[8]

He was plastered.

"What's that you're singing? You've got the rhythm all wrong!" yelled my colleague, gesticulating and spilling his drink all over the tablecloth.

He was drunk too.

"Encore! Encore!" commanded Liu, pointing his chopsticks—which had noodles dangling from them— at his boss. He was bellowing. He was drunk too!

The boss was not offended. He was wobbling as though he could not find his balance. "What do you mean 'encore'?" he said, shaking his head and laughing. "I can't carry a tune. My voice has sounded like a duck's ever since I was a child down on the farm. Whenever the ducks in the river heard my voice, they would all start quacking—"

Instead of being embarrassed by the boss's self-mockery, we all burst out laughing. Liu insisted that the boss sing an encore. My colleague was laughing so hard he was crying, as though he had been making fun of a foolish friend.

The boss was laughing hardest of all. He had loosened his collar, revealing the flushed skin of his neck. He really did sound like a duck. He was rocking with laughter. Then he lost his balance and plopped down into his chair.

"What's your voice like?" he challenged me. "I'll bet you sound like a donkey braying." He laughed, opening his mouth so wide I could see his tonsils.

I felt feverish. I was seized with the urge to be rowdy, to do something I would ordinarily never dare to do. On the spur of the moment I gave the boss a shove.

"Go on! Let's hear *you* bray!" I said.

I almost pushed him off his chair. His glass fell onto the floor. I had just enough sense left to feel vaguely apprehensive. But he merely leaned over and said, "My dear boy, why did you push me so hard? Do you—do you want to—to overthrow me again—and do you—want to—to 'step on'⁹ me again? Well—I'm not afraid of you. Those days are gone—" He brought his face closer to mine. "Do I seem drunk to you?"

His face was practically pressed against mine. I could feel his alcoholic breath on my tingling cheeks. Suddenly I had the hazy sensation that he had been transformed into someone else. He was no longer solemn and forbidding. His face was rosy, as if illuminated by the setting sun. With his silver hair and the delicate curved wrinkles at his eyes and mouth, he now seemed like a kindly old grandfather. I stared at him as through a fog, free of the inhibitions that had constrained me before. I felt so comfortable and relaxed that I had no need of flattery, decorum, tact, or affectation. There were no limits. Everyone was equal, and I could do as I pleased. I was floating heavenward. . . .

What was happening to me?

I racked my sodden brain for some explanation. Maybe this was all like a dream: logical enough while you're asleep, but absurd once you're awake. Was liquor really so magical it could tear down insurmountable barriers of rank and bring out your true personality? Then it was indispensable, I decided. Everyone should get drunk once and enjoy equality, sincerity, and human contact, even if afterward everything reverted back to normal, as it did in fairy tales.

Liquor was wonderful!

Pouring myself another glass, I lurched impulsively to my feet and shouted, "Come on, let's have another round!"

The Street-sweeping Show

"National Cleanup Week starts today," said Secretary Zhao, "and officials everywhere are going out to join in the street sweeping. Here's our list of participants—all top city administrators and public figures. We've just had it mimeographed over at the office for your approval."

He looked like a typical upper-echelon secretary: the collar of his well-worn, neatly pressed Mao suit was buttoned up military style; his complexion was pale; his glasses utilitarian. His gentle, deferential manner and pleasantly modulated voice concealed a shrewd, hard-driving personality.

The mayor pored over the list, as if the eighty names on it were those of people selected to go abroad. From time to time he glanced thoughtfully at the high white ceiling.

"Why isn't there anyone from the Women's Federation?" he asked.

Secretary Zhao thought for a moment. "Oh, you're right—there isn't! We've got the heads of every office in the city—the Athletic Committee, the Youth League Committee, the Federation of Trade Unions, the Federation of Literary and Art Circles—even some famous university professors. The only group we forgot is the Women's Federation."

"Women are the pillars of society. How can we leave out the women's representatives?" The mayor sounded smug rather than reproachful. Only a leader could think of everything. This was where true leadership ability came into play.

Secretary Zhao was reminded of the time when the mayor had pointed out that the fish course was missing from the menu for a banquet in honor of some foreign guests.

"Add two names from the Women's Federation, and make sure you get people in positions of authority or who are proper representatives of the organization. 'March 8 Red Banner Pacesetters,'[1] 'Families of Martyrs,' or 'Model Workers' would be fine." Like an elementary school teacher returning a poor homework paper to his student, the mayor handed the incomplete list back to his secretary.

"Yes, your honor, I'll do it right away. A complete list will be useful the next time something like this comes up. And I must contact everyone at once. The street sweeping is scheduled for two this afternoon in Central Square. Will you be able to go?"

"Of course. As mayor of the city, I have to set an example."

"The car will be at the gate for you at one-thirty. I'll go with you."

"All right," the mayor answered absentmindedly, scratching his forehead and looking away.

Secretary Zhao hurried out.

At one-thirty that afternoon the mayor was whisked to the square in his limousine. All office workers, shop clerks, students, housewives, and retirees were out sweeping the streets, and the air was thick with dust. Secretary Zhao hastily rolled up the window. Inside the car there was only a faint, pleasant smell of gasoline and leather.

At the square they pulled up beside a colorful assortment of limousines. In front of them a group of top city administrators had gathered to wait for the mayor's arrival. Someone had arranged for uniformed policemen to stand guard on all sides.

Secretary Zhao sprang out of the limousine and opened the door for his boss. The officials in the waiting crowd stepped forward with smiling faces to greet the mayor. Everyone knew him and hoped to be the first to shake his hand.

"Good afternoon—oh, nice to see you—good afternoon—" the mayor repeated as he shook hands with each of them.

An old policeman approached, followed by two younger ones pushing wheelbarrows full of big bamboo brooms. The·old policeman selected one of the smaller, neater brooms and presented it respectfully to the mayor, like a Tibetan offering a *hada*² to an honored guest. When the other dignitaries had gotten their brooms, a marshal with a red armband led them all to the center of the square. Naturally the mayor walked at the head.

Groups of people had come from their workplaces to sweep the huge square. At the sight of this majestic, broom-carrying procession, with its marshal, police escort, and retinue of shutter-clicking photographers, they realized that they were in the presence of no ordinary mortals and gathered closer for a look. How extraordinary for a mayor to be sweeping the streets, thought Secretary Zhao, swelling with unconscious pride as he strutted along beside the mayor with his broom on his shoulder.

"Here we are," the marshal said when they had reached the designated spot.

All eighty-two dignitaries began to sweep.

The swelling crowd of onlookers, which was kept back by a police cordon, was buzzing with excitement:

"Look, he's the one over there."

"Which one? The one in black?"

"No. The bald fat one in blue."

"Cut the chitchat!" barked a policeman.

The square was so huge that no one knew where to sweep. The concrete pavement was clean to begin with; they pushed what little grit there was back and forth with their big brooms. The most conspicuous piece of litter was a solitary popsicle wrapper, which they all pursued like children chasing a dragonfly.

The photographers surrounded the mayor. Some got down on one knee to shoot from below, while others ran from side to side trying to get a profile. Like a cloud in a thunderstorm, the mayor was constantly illuminated by silvery flashes. Then a man in a visored cap, with a video camera, approached Secretary Zhao.

"I'm from the TV station," he said. "Would you please ask them to line up single file so they'll look neat on camera?"

Secretary Zhao consulted with the mayor, who agreed to this request. The dignitaries formed a long line and began to wield their brooms for the camera, regardless of whether there was any dirt on the ground.

The cameraman was about to start shooting, when he stopped and ran over to the mayor.

"I'm sorry, your honor," he said, "but you're all going to have to face the other way because you've got your backs to the sun. And I'd also like the entire line to be reversed so that you're at the head."

"All right," the mayor agreed graciously, and he led his entourage, like a line of dragon dancers, in a clumsy turnaround. Once in place, everyone began sweeping again.

Pleased, the cameraman ran to the head of the line, pushed his cap up, and aimed at the mayor. "All right," he said as the camera started to whir, "swing those brooms. All together now—put your hearts into it—

that's it! Chin up please, your honor. Hold it—that's fine—all right!"

He stopped the camera, shook the mayor's hand, and thanked him for helping an ordinary reporter carry out his assignment.

"Let's call it a day," the marshal said to Secretary Zhao. Then he turned to the mayor. "You have victoriously accomplished your mission," he said.

"Very good—thank you for your trouble," the mayor replied routinely, smiling and shaking hands again.

Some reporters came running up to the mayor. "Do you have any instructions, your honor?" asked a tall, thin, aggressive one.

"Nothing in particular." The mayor paused for a moment. "Everyone should pitch in to clean up our city."

The reporters scribbled his precious words in their notebooks.

The policemen brought the wheelbarrows back, and everyone returned the brooms. Secretary Zhao replaced the mayor's for him.

It was time to go. The mayor shook hands with everyone again.

"Good-bye—good-bye—good-bye—"

The others waited until the mayor had gotten into his limousine before getting into theirs.

The mayor's limousine delivered him to his house, where his servant had drawn his bathwater and set out scented soap and fresh towels. He enjoyed a leisurely bath and emerged from the bathroom with rosy skin and clean clothes, leaving his grime and exhaustion behind him in the tub.

As he descended the stairs to eat dinner, his grandson hurriedly led him into the living room.

"Look, Granddad, you're on TV!"

There he was on the television screen, like an actor, putting on a show of sweeping the street. He turned away and gave his grandson a casual pat on the shoulder.

"It's not worth watching. Let's go have dinner."

NOTES

The Mao Button

1. Loyalty to the thought of Chairman Mao, to Chairman Mao's revolutionary road, and to Chairman Mao himself.
2. In China, people take turns serving as neighborhood treasurer.

Chrysanthemums

1. A heatable brick bed platform.
2. A line from "Ballad of the Lute," by the Tang poet Bai Juyi.
3. Zhong Ziqi, of the Zhou dynasty, was the archetypal "appreciative friend." When his friend Bo Ya played the zither, Zhong Ziqi could always tell what the music expressed.
4. The Dunhuang caves, the most famous of which are called the Mogao Caves, are located in Gansu Province. They date from the fourth century A.D. and are renowned for their Buddhist statues, frescoes, and valuable manuscripts.
5. A Neolithic culture that extended across North China, noted for its production of pottery with striking painted decorations.
6. Six bas-reliefs, over five feet high, depicting the favorite steeds of the Tang dynasty Emperor Taizong.
7. From the second century A.D., near Jiaxiang in Shandong Province.
8. The most famous horse painter of the Tang dynasty.

9. A Tang dynasty painter of oxen.
10. A Qing dynasty painter, noted for bamboos and flowers.
11. The prefix Lao (old) is a familiar form of address for one's elders.

Numbskull

1. Sums of money are given throughout this book in Chinese "dollars" (*yuan*). The March 1983 exchange rate was 1.96 *yuan* for 1 U.S. dollar, but a simple numerical conversion does not convey a sense of the value of money in China, where the per capita yearly income in 1980 was $566 U.S.

A Letter

1. This translation represents about four-fifths of the original short novel. The opening and the epilogue have been omitted.

   The story takes place in the late 1960s, during the Cultural Revolution. Wu Zhongyi, a historian in his late thirties, finds himself in danger of being reported to the authorities for dissident remarks he made during the Hundred Flowers Movement, a brief period of relative intellectual and artistic freedom in 1956 and early 1957. At that time Wu openly criticized the state system at a private study group meeting of his elder brother's friends. When the Hundred Flowers Movement was abruptly terminated by the Antirightist Campaign in June 1957, those who had spoken out were branded as rightists and punished. Wu's brother was banished to Manchuria. Wu escaped punishment because he was too shy to broadcast his views beyond the confines of the study group. But another member of the group, Chen Naizhi, repeated Wu's ideas publicly, took credit for them, and was therefore punished instead of Wu.

   As the story opens, Wu receives a letter from his brother warning him that Chen is about to crack under pressure and reveal that Wu was the actual source of the offending views.
2. Shabby clothes were considered a sign of proletarian values.
3. Work teams were ad hoc committees appointed in all workplaces to lead the campaigns of the Cultural Revolution.
4. This character has an implausible name in Chinese that is meant

to indicate his personality. "Lieman" is a translation of it rather than a transliteration.

5. A mandatory daily ceremony during the Cultural Revolution. Participants stood before a portrait of Chairman Mao, recited portions of *Quotations from Chairman Mao*, and wished Chairman Mao longevity.

6. Interest was paid by the state to the national bourgeoisie on the value of their assets after the conversion of private enterprises into state-private concerns in 1956.

7. The personnel section, which keeps dossiers on everyone, is to be feared during a political crackdown.

8. "White terror" is a reference to the bloody suppression of Communists by the Guomindang in the late 1920s.

Winding Brook Way

1. The Summer Palace, located northwest of Beijing, was the summer residence of the imperial court. It is now a park.

2. Harmony Garden (*Xiequ Yuan*) is a famous garden in the Summer Palace.

3. A nine-hundred-yard passageway decorated with landscapes and scenes from history and mythology. It is one of the major attractions of the Summer Palace.

Plum Blossoms in the Snow

1. Three painters known for their depictions of plum blossoms, from the Song, Ming, and Qing dynasties, respectively.

2. A turn-of-the-century artist of the Shanghai school, known for his bold flower paintings.

3. A Qing painter known for his landscapes, orchids, and bamboos.

4. A seventeenth-century landscape painter.

5. See note 7 to "Nectar."

6. Zhao, an ultraleftist, considers the relatively moderate policies from 1949 to 1966 counterrevolutionary.

7. Turning one's back to the sun implies a counterrevolutionary stance.

8. Here Zhao echoes Jiang Qing, who in 1973 criticized the painter

Li Keran for using too much black ink, thereby creating "black" (i.e., counterrevolutionary) paintings.

9. A famous slogan of Mao Zedong.

10. On May 7, 1966, Chairman Mao issued the "May Seventh directive," based on which the "May Seventh cadre schools" were established for the "reeducation" of intellectuals in the countryside. "Five-seven" means "May seventh" in Chinese; hence the rebus.

11. A campaign against Deng Xiaoping in the early spring of 1976.

12. A Q, the most famous fictional character created by the twentieth-century author Lu Xun, is remembered for a complex of personality faults known as A Qism, among which is the tendency to claim "spiritual victory" even when obviously defeated.

13. A seventeenth-century landscape painter.

Nectar

1. A reference to the Cultural Revolution.

2. A reference to the forced retirement of officials during the Cultural Revolution.

3. In China only the highly privileged have enough living space for a separate dining room.

4. At Chinese meals the food is not served on individual plates but set in the center of the table. In formal situations, Chinese table manners require that the guest wait for the host to serve him or to offer him the food.

5. The legendary winebibber Liu Ling was a member of a group of third-century apolitical intellectuals called the Seven Sages of the Bamboo Grove, famous for their meetings in a bamboo grove near the capital where they discussed philosophy over wine.

6. Three of the most famous kinds of Chinese liquor.

7. Guan Gong is an honorific title of Guan Yu (A.D. 162–220), one of the most renowned military heroes in Chinese history. The redness of his face is legendary. He served under Liu Bei, ruler of the kingdom of Shu Han and legitimate claimant to the throne during the Three Kingdoms period of civil war after the fall of the Han dynasty.

8. Qiao Guolao was military adviser to Sun Quan, who led the kingdom of Wu during the Three Kingdoms period. Qiao's aria is a warning to Sun not to underestimate his adversary Liu

Bei, because Liu has Guan Yu (ennobled as marquis of Hanshou) as a sworn brother.

9. A reference to a Cultural Revolution chant encouraging the overthrow of officials:

> *Down with ——— !*
> *Step on him,*
> *And don't let him rise again!*

The Street-sweeping Show

1. March 8 is International Working Women's Day.
2. A piece of silk used in Tibet as a gift of greeting.